Deliver Us From
ABORTION

Deliver Us From
ABORTION

Awakening the Church to End the Killing of America's Children

Brian Fisher

BROWN
CHRISTIAN
A DIVISION OF
BROWN BOOKS PUBLISHING
PRESS

Deliver Us From Abortion
Awakening the Church to End the Killing of America's Children

The *New American Standard Bible* (NASB) is used for biblical quotations, unless otherwise noted.

Brown Christian Press
16250 Knoll Trail Drive, Suite 205
Dallas, Texas 75248
www.BrownChristianPress.com
(972) 381-0009

A New Era in Publishing™

ISBN 978-1-61254-205-8
LCCN 2014952698

Printed in the United States
10 9 8 7 6 5 4 3 2 1

For more information or to contact the author, please go to
www.DeliverUsFromAbortion.com.

In the early 1970s, a baby girl was born in South Korea. Though little is known about the first few years of her life, she eventually ended up in a Korean orphanage. When she was four years old, she was rescued through adoption from what was likely a poverty-stricken lonely life by a caring Christian family in Pittsburgh, PA. That young girl grew in grace, beauty, faith, and love, eventually heading off to college to study elementary education so she could become a teacher, investing her life in the lives of others. It was there we first met, and it was there we fell in love.

After nearly twenty years of marriage, I am more in love and more grateful for Jessica than ever before. She could have been aborted by her biological parents in Korea, but they chose life. She could have been left in the orphanage, but her adopted parents saved her from a life of dangerous uncertainty. And as she will be the first to tell you, Jesus Christ saved her, adopting her into the family of God.

I am blessed beyond measure because of Jessica. I am extraordinarily grateful to her biological parents, who gave her life, and to Dan and Nancy Headrick, who gave her a family. And I dedicate this book to Jess, my wife and best friend, whose very presence at my side is a constant reminder that God is the author of every life, and every life has priceless value and unlimited potential.

Contents

A Personal Note to Parents or Relatives of Aborted Children

For several years now I have worked to rescue children and families from abortion, and I know that an enormous number of men and women in America are parents of aborted children. Millions of others are brothers, sisters, grandparents, aunts, and uncles of those same unborn babies. You may be one of those people.

Abortion remains an incredibly difficult topic to discuss in church, primarily because of its incorrectly politicized characterization, but also due to the guilt, shame, remorse, and sorrow inflicted on parents and relatives.

Writing a book that deals with abortion and the church is a bit of a tightrope act. On one hand, I believe the American church is significantly responsible for abortion's perpetuation, and we deserve the severest of indictments. Professing Christians are supposed to be the protectors of life, but we have abdicated our role.

On the other hand, I want to urgently convey to parents and other relatives of aborted children that there is full, joyous, and freeing forgiveness through Jesus Christ. Christ came to redeem us, and that redemption most certainly includes the sin of abortion.

If you are the parent of an aborted child, you have forgiveness through Christ if you trust in Him and ask Him for that forgiveness. You can be set free from the guilt of abortion.

While I treat the topic of abortion and the church with directness, candor, and not a small amount of frustration, I also have a deep concern for you. My hope and prayer is that you finish this book with a renewed sense of Christ's work in your life and a passionate desire to help stop this unspeakable tragedy.

I am a sinner saved by grace and, like you, need the gospel every day. Let's link arms, experience anew the matchless forgiveness of Jesus, and prayerfully seek the Lord's will as we work to awaken the passive American church—this "sleeping giant"—together.

—**Brian Fisher**

Acknowledgments

To John Aman and Kari Buddenberg, for your research, ideas, editing, reviews, candor, and input: this book would not have been completed without you and is a far better work because of your dedication to its message.

To the staff and volunteers at Online for Life: thank you for your day-in, day-out commitment to the unborn and their families. Your optimism, courage, compassion, and resilience are a continual inspiration to me. You make it easy to come to work each day. Well, most days.

To the Online for Life board of directors: I'm deeply grateful for your service, prayers, wisdom, and counsel. It is a joy to labor with you in this work.

To Milli, Jason, Chesle, and the rest of the great team at Brown Books and Brown Christian Press: thanks for your fantastic work on this project and your passion for life.

To Dr. Tim Boswell for your thoughtful, precise editing: your personal insights and professional pen were just what this book needed.

To Jessica, Caleb, and Zach: I never really wanted to write a book, but it seems God had other plans, as this is number four. Thanks for your love, patience, and support through the necessary struggles in writing books.

This work contains a large amount of biblical material, study, and contemplation. Though I've been a follower of Christ my entire life, I am a layman and, as such, sought input and counsel from a wide range of theologians, church leaders, and academicians. I'm deeply indebted to each of the following co-laborers for their time, constructive criticism, biblical input, and insightful questions. Thank you for improving this book greatly from its original manuscript:

Rev. Geoff Ashley, groups pastor, The Village

Shadia Hrichi, pro-life speaker and author of *Worthy of Love: Finding Hope after Abortion*

Rev. Dean Nelson, founding member of the National Black Pro-Life Coalition and national outreach director of Online for Life

Rev. Clint Patronella, groups pastor at The Village Church, Dallas Northway Campus

Fr. Frank Pavone, national director of Priests for Life and president of National Pro-Life Religious Council

Rev. Jamie Peterson, associate pastor, Christ Presbyterian Church (PCA), Oxford, Mississippi

Dr. Larry Pettegrew, dean and professor of theology, Shepherds Theological Seminary

Dave Sterrett, national director of church outreach, Online for Life

Dr. Anthony Vento, public outreach associate for Priests for Life

To Richard Fisher, my father: though I'm thankful for your careful review of this book (twice), I'm particularly grateful for your consistent encouragement. And to my mother, Janice Fisher, for your faithful prayers.

Introduction

"If you are slack in the day of distress, your strength is limited. Deliver those who are being taken away to death, and those who are staggering to slaughter, Oh hold them back!

If you say, 'See, we did not know this,' does He not consider it who weighs the hearts? And does He not know it who keeps your soul? And will He not render to man according to his work?"

—Proverbs 24:10-12

On a cool, bright evening in October 1999, I sat in Magee-Women's Hospital in Pittsburgh, Pennsylvania, holding my newborn son.

The last few months of his journey to birth had been challenging. His mother, my wife, had been to the hospital six times in the previous few weeks for problems related to preeclampsia. Her blood pressure had to be taken several times a day, and whenever it spiked, another trip to Magee ensued. Those trips resulted in tests, tests, and more tests; concerned looks and furtive discussions among doctors and nurses; poking and prodding; and instructions for limited activity, bed rest, and fluids.

Just a day before, the hospital had attempted to induce labor but failed. My wife struggled through ten hours of labor pains but, because of a miscommunication between doctors, her water wasn't broken, and our little boy remained safely tucked away in her womb.

The second attempt on October 28 was successful, but two successive labors had taken a toll on my wife, and she lay in bed exhausted.

I wasn't really a "kid person." I was in my mid-twenties and hadn't given a second thought to infants for the past two decades. I avoided nurseries (too much crying and strange smells), thought kids were messy, and quickly moved on when I passed a screaming toddler at the mall. I had never changed a diaper and never wanted to. I thought babysitting was for teenage girls and naptime was for Sunday afternoon post-lunch football games.

So I sat there, holding this little baby, wondering what in the world I had gotten myself into.

His mother smiled softly from her hospital bed. My son, Caleb, slept quietly in my arms. And me?

I was terrified.

Men often say that their child's birth is the happiest day of their lives. Not me. What I had just witnessed was beyond my imagination and not particularly pleasant.

When the moment for our special delivery came, every other baby in the hospital decided to come at the same time. Our delivery room was short a few key nurses, so I was recruited to "help" in ways a new father should never have to help.

I had a firsthand, close-up, in-depth perspective of the delivery of a newborn child, and I could only marvel at the messy, bizarre process God designed to bring a life into the world. Surely He could have created a cleaner way to spring forth a new human being.

I was mulling over these thoughts that evening in October after the chaos had subsided, replaying what I had just experienced. Because of the confusion, the delivery was a bit of a blur: nurses running in and out, doctors scrambling in preparation, equipment flying all over the room. Orderlies giving me orders—"Stand here," "Hold this," "Tell her that," "Make sure you don't do that," "Do you want to see this?" ("No").

Nine months of pregnancy, multiple doctor visits, seven emergency trips to the hospital, two labors, hundreds of thousands of dollars' worth of equipment, dozens of doctors and nurses, and two worn-out parents—just to bring a tiny baby into the world.

Caleb was now here, sleeping softly in my arms, oblivious to the miracle of delivery that he had just endured.

He has it easy, I recall thinking. *He won't remember what just happened.*

And then, just for a moment, I had another thought.

We abort him.

Those are the exact words that came to my mind. "We," American men and women, abort "him," little boys and girls. I was holding a tiny baby, my son, and though he was allowed to be born, I realized that there was no difference between him and the millions of other tiny babies that are aborted in their mothers' wombs. This was the first time I had held an hours-old child, and for some reason, the reality of abortion hit home.

I had never given abortion much thought until that moment. I knew abortion existed, and I had some faint inclination of what it was. I was a Christian, and I had a strong conviction that abortion was wrong, though I probably couldn't have articulated why. I didn't recall abortion being talked about in church very often (if at all), and I assumed the Bible had something to say about it, though I couldn't have told you what that was.

Sitting there in the hospital, holding this little boy, my son, the reality of abortion hit home. This little baby is what we are killing. I didn't know how many, I didn't know how often, but I knew it was happening.

And, as quickly as it came, the thought left. I returned to my new-father state of terror.

Thankfully, all was well with Jessica and Caleb, and a few days later, we went home to start our new adventure as a young family.

Years would pass before I became more aware of what abortion is, how often it occurs, and the impact it has on parents, families, and communities. I became involved with a local crisis pregnancy center and started to educate myself. I was horrified by what I learned. Not only was the abortion surgery a gruesome, barbaric process, but I was astounded by how frequently it occurred.

I assumed the entire American church was intimately, aggressively involved in the effort to defend unborn life and protect families from abortion.

I was wrong.

This book represents a very personal journey for me. I have been a Christian since the age of six, so I have often found myself living in the so-called "Christian bubble." I grew up in strong, biblical churches. My parents, my brother, and his family are committed Christians. My upbringing was stable, fruitful, and positive. Most of the companies and organizations I have worked for were family-oriented, faith-based, and energetic.

I love Jesus. I love His church. I have experienced the profound blessing of being raised in a godly home and being part of strong Christian communities.

And so it was with surprise, shock, dismay, and even horror that I discovered that the American church, on the whole, is not actively defending and protecting innocent life. And in some cases, the church actually promotes abortion.

In many churches, abortion is never mentioned from the pulpit. If abortion is discussed at all, it is once a year on Sanctity of Life Sunday, the sad reminder of the anniversary of *Roe v. Wade*.

It is rare to find post-abortive recovery and healing ministries in churches, and almost all of them are for women. Support for post-abortive men is virtually nonexistent.

Precious few pastors or priests write about abortion, and few will publicly defend the unborn. Most denominations have no organized effort to assist families in a crisis pregnancy.

Though a child dies every twenty-five seconds in America due to abortion, God's family, the church, appears ambivalent. We talk about evangelism, but we don't understand the full scope of the gospel. We talk about caring for the poor, but we neglect the frailest members of the human race. We talk about healing, but we ignore the post-abortive, grieving parents sitting next to us in the pews.

I continue to struggle with a haunting question: Why do we, as followers of the Creator God, often refuse to protect His image-bearers?

Why do we, as followers of the God-Man who showed the most precious grace and compassion to women, allow our own wives and girlfriends to be destroyed from the inside out by the deadliest crisis our country has ever faced?

Why do we, as people who say we want to live like the Christ of the Bible, who welcomed children with open arms, permit the arms and legs of our own children to be torn from their tiny bodies in the name of choice?

This project has, at times, caused me to doubt myself and the strength of my commitment to the unborn. It has caused me to doubt the American church, even my own denomination. I have often won-dered about the relevancy of the institution of the church in a culture that is increasingly hostile to it.

Writing this book has forced me to scour the Scriptures, digging into its depths to discover what the Bible does and does not teach about abortion and life in the womb.

I've been brought to the point of tears numerous times, realizing that our nation is in the middle of a torrential downpour of death, and those who are called to sacrificially protect life appear oblivious to the raging storm.

Thankfully, there are Christians working hard to stop abortion in America. There are activists, politicians, lobbyists, pregnancy center staff and volunteers, media experts, writers, bloggers, doctors, nurses, lawyers, and counselors doing wonderful work in the areas where God has called them. They work tirelessly to save babies and restore our culture to one that treasures life.

There are those precious pastors and priests who refuse to stay silent, actively engaging in pro-life work. They preach about abortion from the pulpit, and not just on Sanctity of Life Sunday. The John Pipers, Fr. Frank Pavones, Matt Chandlers, Al Mohlers, John Ensors, Tony Evans, Randy Alcorns, and others of this country have my profound gratitude and respect. They understand that abortion permeates all aspects of life in America. They recognize that abortion is, at its core, a spiritual issue, and thus the Christian church is obligated to address it regularly, vigorously, compassionately, and directly. They realize that the solution to abortion is Christ.

By "Christ," however, I don't mean some flippant Americanized version of Jesus who saves us from hell and gives us stuff if we live right.

I mean the Christ of the Bible. The incomparable Christ, unequaled in all time and space. The Christ who is "the image of the invisible God, the firstborn of all creation. For by Him all things were created, both in the heavens and on earth, visible and invisible, whether thrones or dominions or rulers or authorities—all things have been created through Him and for Him" (Col. 1:15–16).

Though the journey of writing this book has been frustrating at times, it has also instilled in me a profound and enduring hope. And while sometimes I have found it difficult to trust the church, I have grown in my trust of Christ. I see the deadly failings of men. I see the conquering power of our Lord. I see parents exercising fatal power over the innocent and frail. I see Jesus Christ, who bade the children come to Him, restoring, renewing, and redeeming people across our country.

And I believe with every fiber of my being that, through Christ, we can see the end of abortion in America in my lifetime.

This book, this personal journey through the Bible and the church, is separated into three sections. The first section is a primer on abortion and its impact on our culture. I believe millions of Christians are uninformed about the basics of the abortion procedure and how its effects ripple through the entirety of American life. In order to confront abortion scripturally, we need to understand what abortion is. The second section presents a simple, three-part logical argument (an apologetic) based on Scripture and showing why all human life is sacred and to be protected. In the third section, I compare and contrast various denominational doctrines and actions with what the Bible clearly teaches. Then I suggest seven crucial ways we can awaken the church together by the power of the Holy Spirit.

My first son's birthday, October 28, 1999, was the beginning of a long adventure for me. That journey would eventually lead me into full-time, life-affirming work rescuing children and families from abortion. And it has led me to conclude that, without the church, abortion will continue to be a plague on America. But if the church arises, we can work together to end abortion and do so quickly.

I pray that today will be the beginning of your journey, too. I pray the Holy Spirit will awaken your mind and heart to the reality we live in. I pray that He will drive His Word deep in your soul, motivating and urging you to protect and defend the unborn, their families, and the very fabric of American society.

Our nation needs your commitment. Our faith demands it.

Note: I use the term "abortion" in this book as it is culturally accepted, referring exclusively to "elective abortion." While the generic term "abortion" can also refer to an "unintentional" or "spontaneous" abortion, "miscarriage" is commonly used to describe that type of abortion.

Unless otherwise stated, the term "abortion" in this book refers to the willful killing of an innocent, unborn human life, and does not refer to an unintentional miscarriage.

Also, I generally use the word "church" to describe anyone who has professed faith in Jesus Christ, whether that person is Protestant or Catholic. While I realize there are doctrinal and semantic differences in the way each group uses the word "church," for simplicity's sake, I use the term broadly for anyone who follows Christ.

PART 1
Abortion 101

CHAPTER 1
Apathy and Death

B ernard Nathanson understood abortion better than almost any other American. He had expansive experience as a Manhattan ob-gyn in the 1960s, treating women who were "the victims of self-abortion and hack abortionists."[1] Nathanson believed abortion should be legalized in order to spare women the pain and suffering caused by unlicensed abortionists and poor surgical conditions. He cofounded the National Association to Repeal Abortion Laws in 1969 and was a leading figure in the legalization of abortion. Nathanson also directed the largest abortion clinic in the world, presiding over some sixty thousand abortions, including taking the life of his own child.

And then he underwent a radical transformation. Nathanson's attention shifted in 1973 to the medical and scientific facts about the unborn child. He took a good long look at the "intrauterine patient" visible on "the flickering images on an ultrasonic screen."[2] This highly intelligent, educated doctor was moved by the image of a baby in the womb, his heart was changed, and he spent the rest of his days working to end the very thing he helped start.

The abortion doctor became an articulate and impossible-to-ignore advocate for the unborn. His 1984 film, *The Silent Scream*, showed an actual abortion via ultrasound and deeply rattled the abortion industry and the country.

Dr. Nathanson slipped into eternity in 2011, but he left behind a withering assessment of the social phenomenon that has taken the lives of fifty-six million unborn children since 1973. With intimate knowledge of the reality of abortion, having been on both sides of the debate, Nathanson reached this conclusion: "The abortion holocaust is an evil torn free of its moorings in reason and causality, an ordinary secular corruption raised to unimaginable powers of magnification and limitless extremity."[3]

Theologian R. C. Sproul Jr. has said much the same about abortion in America: "You cannot overreact to this problem. This is the most significant, most serious, most dreadful reality in my judgment in the history of the world."[4]

This may seem to be an extreme position on the issue, and it is tempting to write such comments off as hyperbole. Yet as we will see, it is nearly impossible to overstate the depths of this tragedy, the severe loss of life, or the far-reaching impact of abortion on every aspect of society. As the United States Conference of Catholic Bishops said in 1989: "At this particular time, abortion has become the fundamental human rights issue for all men and women of good will. . . . For us, abortion is of overriding concern because it negates two of our most fundamental moral imperatives: respect for innocent life, and preferential concern for the weak and defenseless."[5]

In stark contrast to the great concern behind these statements, many Americans simply don't appear to care about abortion. Yes, a small number of us on both sides are passionate about this issue, but abortion is just a blip on the radar to the rest.

Decades after the Supreme Court's *Roe v. Wade* abortion ruling, most Americans see abortion as no big deal.

Fifty-three percent of us say abortion "is not that important compared to other issues." Another 27 percent say it's one of many important concerns, and just 18 percent see abortion as a critical issue. White evangelicals, statistically the most life-affirming subsection of the American populace, are a bit more concerned, but not much. Just 29 percent see abortion as a critical issue. It's just one among many concerns for 35 percent of white evangelicals. Another 35 percent say it's not a major issue.[6]

Ignorance about abortion may be bliss, but it's also fatal.

Let's be honest—many of us don't want to know. Abortion is an emotionally charged topic with no shortage of vitriol, bitterness, and even hatred. We live in a culture that doesn't want to offend anyone, and the abortion epidemic provokes offense on both sides.

However, just by picking up this book, you're demonstrating that ignorance is not an option for you. And for that, you have my gratitude.

The Basics of Life

Life in the womb is fascinating and breathtaking. Many well-meaning Christians still believe abortion removes a clump of cells from a woman's body. But the miracle of life is far more beautiful and complex.

The "dynamic process by which the single-cell human embryo (called a zygote) becomes a one-hundred-trillion-cell adult is perhaps the most remarkable phenomenon in all of nature," reports the Endowment for Human Development (EHD), a nonprofit organization that claims a position of bioethical neutrality.[7] The more one knows about human development within the womb, the less one can credibly question the humanity of the unborn child at every stage of development, from zygote to embryo to fetus to baby. Here is a quick review from the EHD of what takes place in the first twelve weeks after fertilization, the time of the unborn child's most accelerated growth:

The First 2 Weeks

- The single-cell embryo has a diameter of approximately four-thousandths of an inch.
- The cells of the embryo repeatedly divide as the embryo moves through the Fallopian tube into the woman's uterus.
- Implantation, the process whereby the embryo embeds itself into the wall of the womb, begins by the end of the first week and is completed during the second week of pregnancy.

2 to 4 Weeks

- By 3 weeks, development of the brain, spinal cord, and heart is well underway.
- The heart begins beating at 3 weeks and one day and is visible by ultrasound almost immediately.
- By 4 weeks, the heart is pumping the embryo's own blood to his or her brain and body. All four chambers of the heart are present, and more than one million heartbeats have occurred. The head, chest, and abdominal cavities have formed, and the beginnings of the arms and legs are easily seen.

4 to 6 Weeks

- Rapid brain development continues with the appearance of the cerebral hemispheres at 4½ weeks.
- The embryo reflexively turns away in response to light touch on the face at 5½ weeks.
- Fingers are beginning to form on the hand.

6 to 8 Weeks

- Brainwaves have been measured and recorded before 6½ weeks.

- By 6½ weeks, the bones of the jaw and collarbone begin to harden.

- By 7 weeks, the hands move, the neck turns, and hiccups begin. Girls now have ovaries and boys have testes. The embryo's heart rate peaks at about 170 beats per minute and will gradually slow down until birth.

- By 8 weeks, kidneys begin to produce and release urine, and intermittent breathing motions begin. All fingers and toes are free and fully formed, and several hundred muscles are present. The hands and feet move frequently, and most embryos show the first signs of right- or left-handedness.

- Experts estimate the 8-week-old embryo possesses approximately 90 percent of the 4,500 body parts found in adults. This means that approximately 4,000 permanent body parts are present just eight weeks after conception.

- Incredibly, this highly complex 8-week embryo weighs about one-tenth of an ounce and measures slightly less than 1¼ inches from head to rump.

8 to 10 Weeks

- After 8 weeks, the developing human is called a fetus, which means "little one" or "unborn offspring."

- By 9 weeks, the head moves forward and back, the jaw actively opens and closes, and the fetus periodically sighs and stretches. The face, palms of the hands, and soles of the feet are sensitive to light touch. Thumb sucking and swallowing amniotic fluid begin. Girls' ovaries now contain reproductive cells, which will give rise to eggs later in life. Also in girls, the uterus is now present.

- Yawning begins at 9½ weeks.

- Fingerprints start forming at ten weeks while fingernails and toenails begin to grow.

10 to 12 Weeks

- By 11 weeks, the lips and nose are fully formed, and the fetus can make complex facial expressions.
- By 12 weeks, taste buds are present all over the mouth and tongue.
- The fetus now produces a wide variety of hormones.
- Arms reach final proportion to body size.
- The 12-week fetus weighs about 2 ounces and measures slightly less than 5 inches from head to heel.[8]

Bear in mind that nearly 92 percent of all abortions take place before 13 weeks gestation.[9]

The Reality of Abortion

One of the most striking features of the American abortion debate is that it takes place fairly high on the ladder of abstraction. Even in the church, legal and philosophical matters like the so-called right to privacy, constitutional "penumbras," and whether unborn humans are really "persons" under the law dominate much of the discussion. The harsh reality that abortion violently dismembers a living human being is rarely placed front and center where it belongs.

Understanding abortion procedures is crucial to ending them. As Father Frank Pavone, the head of Priests for Life, says, "America won't reject abortion until it sees abortion."[10]

Planned Parenthood tells young women that the abortion procedure "gently empties your uterus,"[11] but abortion is much more than ending a pregnancy. It is actually a violent and bloody event in which small, defenseless human beings are crushed, dismembered, and suctioned from their mothers.

Let's take a look at the reality of abortion procedures, from surgical to pharmaceutical. And lest we think abortion is somehow less barbaric at earlier stages of fetal development and therefore permissible, pay close attention to the first trimester procedures.

Suction abortion

There are three primary abortion methods employed depending on the age and developmental stage of the unborn child. The most common by far is suction curettage or vacuum aspiration abortion, which is used typically in the first twelve weeks of pregnancy.

Pioneering orthopedic surgeon and former US Surgeon General Dr. C. Everett Koop explains what happens: "A powerful suction tube is inserted through the dilated cervix into the uterus. This tears apart the body of the developing baby and the placenta, sucking the pieces into a jar. The smaller parts of the body are recognizable as arms, legs, head, and so on."[12] Afterward, a curette, described by Koop as a "tiny hoelike instrument," may be used to remove any remaining body parts within the uterus.

About 82 percent of all abortions in the United States are done using this technique, with the vast majority, 74.2 percent, taking place at or before thirteen weeks gestation.[13] The average cost for a surgical abortion at ten weeks is $451, according to the Alan Guttmacher Institute, a pro-abortion research group.[14]

D&E

Dilation and evacuation (D&E) is employed for later abortions up to twenty-five weeks. Planned Parenthood describes the method on its website as follows:

- Your health care provider will examine you and check your uterus.

- You will get medication for pain. You may be offered sedation or IV medication to make you more comfortable.

- A speculum will be inserted into your vagina.

- Your cervix will be prepared for the procedure. You may be given medication or have absorbent dilators inserted a day or a few hours before the procedure. They will absorb fluid and grow bigger. This slowly stretches open your cervix.

- You will be given antibiotics to prevent infection.

- In later second-trimester procedures, you may also need a shot through your abdomen to make sure that the fetus's heart stops before the procedure begins.

- Your health care provider will inject a numbing medication into or near your cervix.

- Medical instruments and a suction machine gently empty your uterus.[15]

Former abortionist Dr. Anthony Levatino gives a more detailed and vivid explanation of what happens in a twenty-week D&E abortion, which cost $1,562 in 2009:[16]

> A second trimester D&E abortion is a blind procedure. The baby can be in any orientation or position inside the uterus. Picture yourself reaching in with the Sopher clamp and grasping anything you can. At twenty weeks gestation, the uterus is thin and soft, so be careful not to perforate or puncture the walls. Once you have grasped something inside, squeeze on the clamp to set the jaws

and pull hard—really hard. You feel something let go and out pops a fully formed leg about 4 to 5 inches long. Reach in again and grasp whatever you can. Set the jaw and pull really hard once again, and out pops an arm about the same length. Reach in again and again with that clamp and tear out the spine, intestines, heart and lungs.[17]

Colorado abortionist Warren Hern told a 1978 Planned Parenthood conference about the "emotional trauma" medical staff experience when they participate in D&E abortions. "We have reached a point in this particular technology where there is no possibility of denial of an act of destruction by the operator," Hern and his coauthor wrote. "It is before one's eyes. The sensations of dismemberment flow through the forceps like an electric current."[18]

Abortion after twenty-five weeks (six months)

Abortionists who commit abortions after twenty-five weeks sometimes use a technique developed by abortionist George Tiller that is done through thirty-five weeks of gestation (babies spend about thirty-eight weeks in the womb). The so-called MOLD technique—an acronym based on the use of misoprostol, oxytocin, laminaria, and digoxin—begins when a lethal dose of digoxin is injected with a long needle into the heart of the baby or into the amniotic sac. This induces a heart attack and kills the child.

Laminaria, thin sticks of seaweed that expand when moistened, are then inserted to open the cervix, and misoprostol is introduced vaginally to prepare the cervix and stimulate contractions. Delivery of the dead baby comes on day three or four. The drug oxytocin is administered on day four to induce contractions and the mothers, in some cases, are taken to a room where they can deliver into a toilet.

You read that correctly. Late-term abortionists sometimes use toilets to "catch" infants when they are expelled from their mothers. And these children are not always dead. A worker at Kermit Gosnell's abortion facility testified during his murder trial that she saw a large baby delivered by his mother into a toilet. The infant struggled in what seemed like a swimming motion as he attempted to get out of the toilet. Another clinic worker took the infant and killed him by cutting his spinal cord as the mother watched while she sat bleeding into the toilet.[19]

The violence I have just described to you takes place on a mass scale. More than 1.2 million infants, most in the first twelve weeks of their young lives, are killed in America every year. The total loss of life from abortion since 1973 is greater than the death toll from all US wars combined and equals nearly 18 percent of the total current US population.

Pharmaceutical abortion

A rapidly growing number of early abortions are now done nonsurgically, using a combination of drugs that first cause the placenta to detach from the uterus and then induce uterine contractions that deliver a dead baby. So-called medical or pharmaceutical abortions have been done in the United States since 2000, when the Food and Drug Administration approved mifepristone (also known as RU-486) for abortions. The drug is used to abort children at seven weeks gestation or younger and now accounts for 16.5 percent of all abortions in the United States, according to statistics from 2009, the last year with reported statistics. The use of mifepristone increased 350 percent from 2001 to 2009[20], and the average cost of a pharmaceutical abortion in 2009 was $483.[21]

The website www.Abort73.com explains that mifepristone works by "prohibiting the synthesis and functionality of progesterone, a hormone that is necessary to sustain early pregnancy. When the role of progesterone is compromised, the uterus contracts, the endometrium becomes hostile to the implanted embryo, and the cervix softens to allow expulsion." Another drug, misoprostol, is used in conjunction with mifepristone to induce contractions that expel the child from the womb.

Pharmaceutical abortions take place over a couple days and begin when the mother swallows the mifepristone pill(s). In 95 percent of instances, the tiny infant will not have been delivered within two days and the mother returns to the abortion facility to obtain misoprostol tablets. She will generally stay at the abortion facility waiting up to four hours for expulsion. Abort73.com reports that the "first large-scale clinical trial of this regimen in the U.S. indicated that 49 percent of women abort within four hours of misoprostol administration and 75 percent abort within 24 hours; the median duration of bleeding is 13 days."[22]

A final step takes place two weeks later when the woman returns to confirm her abortion is complete. If not, a suction abortion is scheduled and completed.

Bad Company

Considering the barbarism of these abortion procedures, it's hard to imagine that an American is aborted every twenty-five seconds. How have we descended to the depths of infanticide where 3,500 of our children are lost to abortion every day?

It's important to understand that American abortion law is permissive in the extreme. While we often claim America as a bastion of human rights and equality, if you are an unborn child, this is one of the last countries on the planet in which you'd want to be conceived.

Only three other nations join the United States in giving mothers an unlimited right to end the young lives growing within them up to and including full-term birth. Only the communist regimes of China and North Korea, along with Canada, share with the United States an abortion culture that permits abortion for any reason after the child is viable outside the womb. Our law has the same disregard for the rights of the unborn as two of the most brutal and authoritarian regimes in the world.

The United States is one of just nine nations that have legalized abortion after fourteen weeks of gestation. Even secular Europe is much stricter than the United States when it comes to abortion, with seventeen of twenty-seven European nations limiting abortion to twelve weeks.[23]

A fairly unknown fact is that the US Supreme Court gave pregnant women the right in 1973 to end their babies' lives for any reason right up to birth. *Doe v. Bolton*, the Court's 1973 companion decision to *Roe v. Wade*, opened the door to abortion for any and all reasons when it allowed abortions for the life and health of the mother and then defined health in the broadest terms possible. Though a number of states have passed tougher laws to limit abortions, the reality is abortion is available on demand with relative ease in many areas of the country.

"Health," as Justice Harry Blackmun explained in *Doe*, is to be defined "in light of all factors—physical, emotional, psychological, familial, and the woman's age—relevant to the well-being of the patient. All these factors relate to health."[24] This is the loophole that makes abortion legal for all nine months of pregnancy.

Ten years after *Roe* and *Doe*, the US Senate Judiciary Committee took a very close look at the Court's abortion rulings and concluded that "no significant legal barriers of any kind whatsoever exist today in the United States for a woman to obtain an abortion for any reason during any stage of her pregnancy."[25]

The result is that abortion now takes one out of every five unborn children in America, and the body count since 1973 tops fifty-six million.

Law professor Joseph Dellapenna, author of a 1,300-page abortion history, states, "The Supreme Court's haste to decide these cases. . .imposed a more extreme approach to abortion on the United States than is found in almost any other nation."[26]

Deadly Confusion

Few Americans understand that "abortion on demand" is the law of the land under the rulings handed down by the high court in *Roe* and *Doe*. A 2006 national poll showed that just 29 percent of Americans know that *Roe* "made abortion legal in essentially all circumstances throughout pregnancy." Fifty percent of those answering the poll said *Roe* limits abortion to early pregnancy or in limited circumstances.[27]

"It's something of a puzzle why the public has never really grasped how extreme the legal treatment of abortion is in the United States," says Harvard law professor Mary Ann Glendon. The sharp disconnect between legal reality and public perception stems in part from distorted media accounts of what the Court did in 1973. The *New York Times*, in its page one next-day account of the Court's January 22, 1973, abortion decisions, told readers "High Court Rules Abortions Legal the First 3 Months."[28] That template for what *Roe* means has been largely undisturbed in the forty years since.

A January 2013 *Wall Street Journal*/NBC poll asked respondents if they wanted *Roe* overturned, telling them that "[t]he Supreme Court's 1973 *Roe versus Wade* decision established a woman's constitutional right to an abortion, at least in the first three months of pregnancy."[29] With the question posed that way, 70 percent opposed reversing *Roe*.

The result would have been sharply different if the question accurately stated that *Roe* and *Doe* together gave women the right to end their child's life right up to delivery. While 61 percent of Americans say abortion should be legal in the first three months of pregnancy, huge majorities of 64 and 80 percent oppose abortions in the second and third trimesters, respectively.[30]

It's not just media misinformation that accounts for our failure to grasp the truth about American abortion law. It's also almost beyond belief, says Glendon, that the Court would "permit the intentional destruction of a healthy infant who was capable of living outside his or her mother's body when the mother's health (in the ordinary meaning of that word) is not in serious danger." But that's what happened. More than four decades later, most Americans still don't know that abortion is legal at any stage of pregnancy according to federal law.

While there have historically been limits on the federal funding of abortions, and states are allowed to ban or restrict abortions at later stages of pregnancy, the fact remains that the United States federal government remains a worldwide leader in abortion permissiveness.

Though American law is extremely permissive of abortion, we could reasonably assume that many Americans are horrified with the procedure. Yet at least some of our ambivalence can be attributed to a lack of media coverage and clear explanation of the procedures.

Pro-abortion reporters who prize the "right to choose" aren't apt to reveal the ugly facts. Alex S. Jones, a former *New York Times* reporter, says, "Reporters as a group tend to be pro-choice, and pro-life advocates have long complained that these biases have skewed the way the story is reported."[31]

Here are a few examples:

- When Congress debated a ban on partial-birth abortion in the late 1990s, many in the media repeated the abortion industry claim that the cruel procedure was a rare event. An investigation by Ruth Padawer at the *Bergen Record* reported some 1,500 partial-birth abortions were done in one year in New Jersey alone. *Washington Post* reporter David Brown then found a similar pattern nationally. "Shockingly—and disappointingly—the other great news organizations generally ignored what Padawer and Brown had found," wrote Jones.[32]

- The media generally refused to show partial-birth abortion diagrams to their audience. Both the *New York Times* and *USA Today* rejected a Focus on the Family ad in 2000 that criticized partial-birth abortion. The ad was in poor taste, according to a *USA Today* spokesman, but conservative columnist George Will called it "censorship."[33]

- Media abortion bias was displayed again in 2013 when journalists generally avoided the trial of late-term abortionist Kermit Gosnell, charged with the murder of infants at his clinic, but celebrated Texas legislator Wendy Davis when she filibustered a bill to ban abortions after twenty weeks. The Media Research Center reported that ABC, CBS, and NBC "devoted 40 minutes, 48 seconds of their morning and evening news programs to stories including Davis" in the nineteen days after her filibuster. They gave just thirteen and a half minutes to Gosnell "during the entire 58 days of the murder trial."[34]

It's not just the media, however. Abortion advocates have carefully hidden the gruesome reality of abortion, and they've done so from the very beginning. A 1970 editorial in *California Medicine*, a journal of the California Medical Association, explained that dishonesty and denial are needed to ease the shift away from the reverence for life that has guided Western medicine. Because the old ethic is not yet gone, the editorial said,

> it has been necessary to separate the idea of abortion from the idea of killing, which continues to be socially abhorrent. The result has been a curious avoidance of the scientific fact, which everyone really knows, that human life begins at conception and is continuous whether intra- or extra-uterine until death. The very considerable semantic gymnastics which are required to rationalize abortion as anything but taking a human life would be ludicrous if they were not often put forth under socially impeccable auspices. It is suggested that this schizophrenic sort of subterfuge is necessary because while a new ethic is being accepted, the old one has not yet been rejected.[35]

The most famous example of semantic gymnastics is the term "pro-choice," which entered the lexicon in the mid-1970s. That now-ubiquitous term for those who in the pre-*Roe* years were uniformly labeled "pro-abortion" was invented by abortion activists to "remake the vocabulary with which Americans talked about abortion," says abortion historian Cynthia Gorney.[36] "Choice" now stands for abortion in the public mind, distracting us from the ugly reality that this choice involves killing another human being.

Candor about the death and dismemberment of an unborn child is almost universally missing from pro-abortion literature. The National

Abortion Federation (NAF), an association of abortion providers, states, "Abortion means you are choosing to end a pregnancy."[37] Planned Parenthood provides an equally sanitized definition, explaining that "[a]bortion is a safe and legal way to end pregnancy."[38]

Nor will you find specific details about the amazing development of the unborn child, such as the fact that the baby's heart starts beating at twenty-one days. Instead, a resource recommended by NAF is critical of "state-prepared booklets on fetal development." These booklets "tend to focus on emotionally charged details of fetal growth—for example, when fingernails and toenails develop."[39]

Abortion as a Way of Life

Forty years after the Supreme Court legalized abortion on demand, the practice is deeply embedded into American life:

- Abortion is one of the most common surgical procedures in the United States.
- It is the leading cause of death (heart disease kills six hundred thousand annually, while over 1.2 million pre-born children die each year from abortion).
- Three in ten women in America are post-abortive by the time they are forty-five. This implies that around 30 percent of men are also post-abortive.
- Abortion is an enormous industry, generating more than $800 million each year for abortion doctors, facilities, and providers.[40] Black market industries exist around the business of abortion.[41]
- Virtually every major city in America has at least one abortion clinic and most large cities have several. New York City is America's abortion capital with 80,485 abortions in 2011.[42] Almost half of New York City's pregnancies end in abortion each year.

- 75 percent of women having abortions offer convenience-related reasons, according to a 2005 study from the Guttmacher Institute.[43]

Abortion is treated as a fallback method of birth control in America, as our nation's highest court acknowledged in 1992 when it upheld *Roe v. Wade*. "For two decades," the Supreme Court ruled, "people have organized intimate relationships and made choices . . . in reliance on the availability of abortion in the event that contraception should fail."[44]

Abortions are also done for reasons other than the woman's health. A 2006 Guttmacher study of hundreds of women who had second-trimester abortions found not one woman who said her abortion was for health reasons.[45]

Abortionist Martin Haskell, regarded as the inventor of the now-illegal, late-term, partial-birth abortion method, told American Medical News in 1993 that "most of my abortions are elective in that 20-24 week range." He estimated that "probably 20 percent are for genetic reasons. And the other 80 percent are purely elective."[46]

Those "genetic reasons" are used, for example, to abort more than 90 percent of Down syndrome babies, infants who have various birth defects due to an extra chromosome.[47] Other children felled by abortion include those afflicted with anencephaly, trisomy 13 and 18, Tay-Sachs disease, spina bifida, and cystic fibrosis. Instead of loving and caring for children with special needs, parents, often pressured by healthcare professionals, are choosing to take the life of their "defective" child and, perhaps, try again.

The faulty premise behind these deaths is that special-needs kids are worth less than other healthy children. Our culture assumes special-needs kids can't have meaningful, productive lives. Yet consider the Martin family.

Sean and Jill Martin had two biological children. They wanted to grow their family, so they looked into adoption. They discovered that special-needs kids are often passed over in favor of healthier children, so they decided to adopt a special-needs child. Then they adopted another, then one more. They picked up multiple special-needs siblings, but they kept looking for more children. As of this writing, the Martins have a total of ten children, eight of which have special needs ranging from Down syndrome to paralysis. Most of their children are victims of fetal alcohol syndrome.

The Martins live on a farm north of Dallas, Texas. They homeschool all ten children, and Sean and Jill have trained the kids to work the farm. They grow much of their own food. A few of their kids will go on to live fairly normal lives, but several of them will be in their parents' care for life.

They are one of the most beautiful families you'll ever meet. All of their children are educated, loved, and productive according to their capabilities. If you told the Martins their special-needs children are worth less than healthier children, they would look at you like you were crazy.

The number of infants with genetic maladies who die via abortion will spike upward as a new blood test known as noninvasive prenatal genetic diagnosis (NIPD) debuts and makes assessing the unborn's genetic fitness much easier and more widespread. *Nature* magazine told readers in 2011 to "[g]et ready for the flood of fetal gene screening."

Forty years after the Court gave us legal abortion, much of our society is now organized around the option of easy abortion when things don't go as planned. This deeply embedded feature of modern

America is part of a societal shift that has been called the "culture of death," a shift toward the devaluation of human life.

It goes beyond devaluation, though. The term "holocaust" can refer to a mass slaughter of people, and out of respect for the Holocaust of World War II, the word should not be used lightly. Yet it is entirely accurate to call the abortion epidemic what it is—an American holocaust. Nine times as many lives have been lost to abortion compared to the concentration camps. The "culture of death" is most readily apparent in this silent holocaust that has killed fifty-six million Americans.

And its true face came to public light when law enforcement officers raided a Philadelphia abortion facility in 2010. They arrived to make a drug bust but found something much more horrific.

CHAPTER 2
The American Holocaust

It was about 8:30 on the evening of February 11, 2010, and Philadelphia abortionist Dr. Kermit Gosnell had just showed up at his abortion facility known as the Women's Medical Society. A team of law enforcement officers were waiting. They were investigating illegal prescription drug activity at his clinic and entered the building with him.

They were stunned by what they found, describing the scene as "filthy," "deplorable," "disgusting," "very unsanitary, very outdated, horrendous," and "by far, the worst" these seasoned professionals had ever seen. According to the grand jury report:

> There was blood on the floor. A stench of urine filled the air. A flea-infested cat was wandering through the facility, and there were cat feces on the stairs. Semi-conscious women scheduled for abortions were moaning in the waiting room or the recovery room, where they sat on dirty recliners covered with blood-stained blankets.[48]

In Gosnell's absence, unlicensed staff had sedated the women but had no record or recollection of dosages or medications. Dead babies were

> haphazardly stored throughout the clinic—in bags, milk jugs, orange juice cartons, and even in cat-food containers. Some fetal remains were in a refrigerator, others were frozen. . . . The investigators found a row of jars containing just the severed feet of fetuses. In the basement, they discovered medical waste piled high.[49]

Gosnell told a detective that 10 to 20 percent of the children were beyond twenty-four weeks gestation—despite a Pennsylvania law that bans abortions after twenty-four weeks.

Gosnell performed late-term abortions by inducing labor and then dispatching the infants by severing the spinal cord, a process the clinic staff called "snipping." "It was literally a beheading," Stephen Masoof, an unlicensed medical school graduate who performed abortions at Gosnell's clinic, said at Gosnell's trial. "It is separating the brain from the body."[50] Many babies were delivered alive and breathing, according to a clinic worker who testified against Gosnell at his trial in 2013. Kareena Cross said she saw at least ten babies born alive and breathing that Gosnell killed by cutting their necks.[51]

Gosnell is now serving a life sentence for the deaths of three infants, but there is plenty of evidence that he killed many more. Lest we think this case is extreme and unique in its horror, the squalor in Gosnell's clinic and his contempt for women and children are more common than we'd like to admit.

Americans United for Life reports that just since 2009, "86 abortion providers in 29 states have faced investigations, criminal charges, civil lawsuits, or administrative complaints for providing substandard patient care or have been cited for violating state abortion laws."[52] Numerous cases show that other abortion facilities exhibit the same disregard for life as Gosnell did.

Two nurses at a Planned Parenthood clinic in Delaware quit their jobs in 2013 and went public with shocking allegations about conditions inside the clinic. "It was just unsafe. I couldn't tell you how ridiculously unsafe it was," said Jayne Mitchell-Werbrich, a former employee. She alleged that an abortionist at the clinic "didn't wear gloves." Another former employee, Joyce Vasikonis, told WPVI-TV in Philadelphia, "They were using instruments on patients that were not sterile." The nurses charged that clinic operating tables were not cleaned between patients. "It's not washed down, it's not even cleaned off," said Mitchell Werbrich. "It has bloody drainage on it." Vasikonis said patients "could be at risk of getting hepatitis, even AIDS."[53]

Authorities in Muskegon, Michigan, found a "filthy mess"[54] and conditions "dangerous to human life or the public welfare" after they entered a local abortion facility to investigate a broken rear window in 2012. An inspection of Dr. Robert Alexander's Women's Medical Services revealed wretched conditions, including blood dripping from a sink trap, "blood on the floor and walls in multiple locations," and "uncovered buckets containing unknown fluids."[55]

Alexander's clinic was shut down, but a Muskegon ob-gyn has urged the state to revoke the doctor's medical license, saying he has had to repair damage done to patients by Alexander. The ob-gyn wrote about one botched abortion on a woman in her second trimester:

Dr. Alexander perforated the woman's uterus so badly that it was hanging on by two blood vessels. The decapitated head of a fetus was in the woman's abdomen and the large intestine had been grasped and pulled away from its blood supply and into the vagina. The woman required a hysterectomy . . . and several units of blood to save her life.[56]

Three former employees of Texas late-term abortionist Douglas Karpen told Operation Rescue that Karpen frequently delivered babies who were twenty weeks and beyond and then killed them by cutting their spinal cord or jamming an instrument into the soft spot on top of the baby's head. On other occasions, he would kill infants by "twisting the head off the neck, kind of, with his own bare hands," said Deborah Edge, who spent fifteen years working for Karpen as a surgical assistant.[57]

The mothers were given misoprostol to induce contractions and sometimes delivered in toilets or, once, in the hallway. "He just picked it up with one of those [disposable] pads and put it in the trash bag," said former employee Krystal Rodriguez of the baby delivered in the hallway.[58]

Operation Rescue researcher Cheryl Sullenger uncovered a 2005 incident in which a sewer break near Karpen's abortion facility spilled raw sewage that included dismembered unborn children into a nearby car dealership's parking lot. Maribeth Smith, who worked at the dealership, took photos and said, "Whether it's legal or not, it's not right. This whole area is nothing but raw sewage and bloody pieces. There were little legs coming out from one side."[59]

The pro-life group Live Action has released undercover videos in which other late-term abortionists admit they will allow live newborns to die. Washington, DC abortionist Cesare Santangelo told a Live Action undercover investigator what he would do if her twenty-four-week-old baby survived the abortion:

> Let's say you went into labor, the membranes ruptured, and you delivered before we got to the termination part of the procedure here, you know? Then we would do things—we would—we would not help it. We wouldn't intubate. It would be, you know, uh, a person, a terminal person in the hospital, let's say, that had cancer, you know? You wouldn't do any extra procedures to help that person survive. Like "do not resuscitate" orders. We would do the same things here.[60]

In another undercover Live Action video, a Bronx, New York abortion counselor explained how a born alive baby would be placed in a toxic "solution" to ensure death. Asked what would happen if the baby were breathing, the counselor explained, "It will automatically stop. It won't be able to breathe anymore. Not in the—not with the solution."[61]

The heartless reality of abortion in America surfaced again in 2013 when a Planned Parenthood lobbyist told stunned Florida lawmakers that the fate of a baby born alive is up to the mother and her doctor.

"So, um, it is just really hard for me to even ask you this question because I'm almost in disbelief," said Rep. Jim Boyd. "If a baby is born on a table as a result of a botched abortion, what would Planned Parenthood want to have happen to that child that is struggling for life?" Planned Parenthood lobbyist Alisa LaPolt Snow responded, "We believe that any decision that's made should be left up to the woman, her family, and the physician."[62]

In other words, no automatic and immediate medical intervention would be implemented to save the newborn baby's life. Instead, the fate of a newborn hinges on whether the mother has a sudden change of heart and decides, along with the abortionist, to reverse course and let the just-delivered child live.

"After a while we begin to disrespect human life in ways that are just shockingly coarse. And that's what happened here," Charles J. Chaput, the Roman Catholic archbishop of Philadelphia, said during the Gosnell trial. "They were treating the babies from the womb as though they were pieces of trash."

Extending the Argument

Chaput said Gosnell is "a consequence of the fact that we have a growing culture of disrespect for human life as a result of the decision of the Supreme Court here those many years ago."[63] As we eliminate the unborn routinely, that culture of disrespect is taking root in more and more hearts and minds. And that means more violence, not less. "If we can treat unborn children this way, it means we're capable of treating born children this way, and the elderly this way," the archbishop said.

Maybe that's overstated. After all, who favors infanticide?

Two Australian ethicists argued in 2012 for what they call "after-birth abortion" in the *Journal of Medical Ethics*, an international peer-reviewed journal read by health professionals and specialists in medical ethics. Alberto Giubilini and Francesca Minerva say the same reasons given for abortion—fetal abnormality and the psychological burden on the mother—can be used to justify killing a child already born. Or, as they put it, "when circumstances occur after birth such that they would have justified abortion, what we call after-birth abortion should be permissible."[64] The article sparked an uproar, but the editor justified its publication by noting that numerous other moral philosophers and ethicists have supported infanticide in the past forty years.

Princeton's Peter Singer is probably the best-known advocate for infant killing. When it comes to infanticide, Singer suggests that "we should put aside feelings based on the small, helpless, and—sometimes—cute appearance of human infants." If we dispense with "these emotionally moving but strictly irrelevant aspects of the killing of a baby, we can see that the grounds for not killing persons do not apply to newborn infants."[65]

Other moral philosophers and thinkers agree:

- Feminist theologian Beverly Harrison, author of the 1983 pro-abortion volume, *Our Right to Choose*, asserted: "Infanticide is not a great wrong. I do not want to be construed as condemning women who, under certain circumstances, quietly put their infants to death."[66]

- Philosopher Michael Tooley announced in 1972 that "human fetuses and infants . . . do not have a right to life" because they "fail to meet the condition an organism must meet if it is to have a serious right to life."[67]

- British bioethicist Jonathan Glover thinks "infanticide is sometimes right."[68] As he sees it, "The objection to infanticide is at most no stronger than the objection to frustrating a baby's current set of desires, say by leaving him to cry unattended for a longish period."[69]

- "I don't think infanticide is always unjustifiable," says John Harris, a bioethics professor at the University of Manchester in England. He sees no moral distinction between born and unborn. "There is no obvious reason why one should think differently, from an ethical point of view, about a fetus when it's outside the womb rather than when it's inside the womb."[70]

- "There is no basis for a radical moral distinction between abortion and infanticide," writes Jeff McMahan, author of *The Ethics of Killing: Problems at the Margins of Life*.[71] That claim, and others, "exert pressure on us either to accept the occasional permissibility of infanticide or to reject liberal beliefs about abortion."[72]

This line of thinking makes sense: If abortion is OK, why not infanticide too? These thinkers are only connecting the dots self-evident to many in the pro-life community a generation ago. "The wide-open door of abortion-on-demand leads naturally to infanticide, which leads naturally to euthanasia," evangelical philosopher Francis Schaeffer and orthopedic surgeon C. Everett Koop warned in 1979.[73]

As West Germany's Federal Constitutional Court said in 1975, when it banned abortion on demand during the first three months of pregnancy, "We cannot ignore the educational impact of abortion on the respect for life."[74]

Half of Americans think it's permissible to abort children with mental or physical impairments, according to a 2011 Gallup poll.[75] Pre-born children with diseases diagnosed in the womb are aborted at a high rate. The *American Spectator* reports that, according to a 2012 review of seventeen international studies, "once prenatal diagnosis is made, anencephaly has an abortion rate of 83 percent and spina bifida of 63 percent." Another earlier review of twenty studies found that the abortion rate is almost 100 percent for children with spina bifida or anencephaly, 74 percent for Turner syndrome, and 92 percent for Down syndrome.[76]

These startling numbers underscore how abortion has made America a less caring nation, one in which impaired unborn children are routinely eliminated.

"We are largely unaware that we have, as a society, already embraced the eugenic principle, 'Defectives shall not be born,' because our practices are decentralized and because they operate not by coercion but by private reproductive choice," says ethicist Leon Kass.[77]

The abortion culture in America is so insidious, it infects and affects our thinking about all life, including life outside the womb.

A Culture of Narcissism and Death

The Bible declares that God is a God of love, joy, peace, and mercy. His church, therefore, is to embody these and numerous other charitable characteristics. We must ask ourselves if the American church is genuinely portraying those life-giving qualities or if we have devolved into promoting a culture opposite of what God instructs.

America and much of the Western world has shifted from a culture of life to what Pope John Paul II called a "culture of death" in his famous 1995 encyclical, *Evangelium Vitae* (The Gospel of Life). A "new cultural climate is developing," the pope wrote, in which "broad sectors of public opinion justify certain crimes against life in the name of the rights of individual freedom, and . . . claim not only exemption from punishment but even authorization by the State, so that these things can be done with total freedom and indeed with the free assistance of healthcare systems."[78]

Others have defined the culture of death as a "powerful secularized culture that dominates both Europe and America today,"[79] and a "naturalistic ethic sweeping across the entire spectrum, from the unborn to the old and infirm, from the deformed and disabled to the weak and defenseless."[80]

The political and legal dimensions of abortion are widely covered in the news, but that only scratches the surface. The true scope of abortion and its impact on individual lives, as well as on our culture, remains almost untouched. Take post-abortion pain, for example—a reality mostly ignored or dismissed by our culture. "The psychological and spiritual agony of abortion is silenced by society, ignored by the media, rebuffed by mental health professionals, and scorned by the women's movement," says Theresa Burke, the founder of Rachel's Vineyard, a ministry that helps men and women find healing after abortion. "Post-abortion trauma is a serious and devastating illness which has no celebrity spokeswoman, no made-for-television movie, and no platform for the talk show confessional."[81]

A huge segment of our population is forced to suffer in silence because of our culture-wide denial of abortion's aftereffects. Yet this is just one consequence of the culture of death. There are many more.

Abortion also unravels the social fabric by licensing a new, manipulative, and utilitarian relationship between men and women. Abortion is an easy out for irresponsible men who get women pregnant and then pressure their girlfriends and wives into abortions. Feminist Alice Paul, the original architect of the Equal Rights Amendment, called abortion the "ultimate exploitation" of women. Paul, like many early feminists of the nineteenth century, was forcefully opposed to abortion.

Young men acutely understand how abortion serves their interests. Texas blogger Sam Sherman lashed out at pending pro-life legislation in Texas, warning of the toll it would take on the sex lives of out-of-control men like him:

> Forcing women to adhere to the anti-choice attitudes of
> state legislators forces men to do the same, and will have

serious consequences both on men's lives and lifestyles. Your sex life is at stake. Can you think of anything that kills the vibe faster than a woman fearing a back-alley abortion? Making abortion essentially inaccessible in Texas will add an anxiety to sex that will drastically undercut its joys. And don't be surprised if casual sex outside of relationships becomes far more difficult to come by.[82]

For Sam and his fellow "bro-choicers," the right to choose is necessary for them to use women for their own rampant sexual satisfaction.

"I really think that abortion is at the root—you could do a flow-chart—I think abortion is at the root of so much that has and is going wrong in this country," says radio talk host Rush Limbaugh, one of the most listened-to men in America. "I think it's almost at the root of everything. And if it's not at the root of everything, it's clearly had a profound impact on our culture, our society, and our politics, I think, in ways that people don't even stop to consider."[83] Rush is absolutely correct. After all, abortion is endemic in American culture. We've lost more than fifty-six million children to abortion since 1973. Nearly one in three women in America will have an abortion by age forty-five,[84] which suggests that an almost-equal number of men will also have one or more abortions in their past.

The culture of death champions a new ethic based on brute force. The "freedom to choose," after all, is nothing more than "the freedom of the strong against the weak, who have no choice but to submit," as the pontiff put it.

At its foundation, the culture of death is in direct opposition to biblical Christianity. It overthrows the high regard for human life promoted and defended by the Christian faith nearly two thousand years ago, which replaced the cruel ethics of ancient Greece and Rome where life was very cheap. "Not only was the exposure of infants [killing a child by leaving him or her out in the elements until death] a very common practice" in the Greco-Roman world, writes historian Rodney Stark, "it was justified by law and advocated by philosophers."[85] Peter Singer observes, "Both Plato and Aristotle recommended the killing of deformed infants." He says Christianity is responsible for the "change in Western attitudes since Roman times to infanticide" and gave us the "doctrine of the sanctity of human life." Singer hopes the time has come to reassess the morality of infanticide "without assuming the Christian moral framework that has, for so long, prevented any fundamental reassessment."[86]

The door is still shut to infanticide as a matter of law, but abortion has already taken a heavy toll on the reverence for life that once distinguished Western civilization. The influential medical journal *California Medicine* stated in 1970 that respect for the "intrinsic worth and equal value of every human life" was a "keystone of Western medicine" that was "being eroded at its core and may eventually even be abandoned." The editors also warned that this "will produce profound changes in Western medicine and in Western society."[87] Writing just as the culture of death began to darken our land, the editors of *California Medicine* spoke of "hard choices" ahead and predicted:

> [i]t will become necessary and acceptable to place relative rather than absolute values on such things as human lives, the use of scarce resources, and the various elements which are to make up the quality of life or of living which is to be sought. This is quite distinctly

at variance with the Judeo-Christian ethic and carries serious philosophical, social, economic, and political implications for Western society and perhaps for world society.[88]

The Christian ethic is to value all human life, and that central point lights the way for the rest of this book. Abortion is primarily a spiritual battle, a clash of worldviews that stems from our beliefs about God, mankind, our purpose, and eternity. The reason "pro-choicers oppose even modest limits [on abortion procedures]," write Charles Colson and Nancy Pearcey, is "because they understand that abortion represents a worldview conflict: God and the sanctity of life versus the individual's moral autonomy. They can give no quarter."[89]

That uncompromising attitude is what I'm concerned is missing from much of today's Christian church. As Christians, we may be tempted to think that abortion is a non-church issue outside of one Sunday in January. Yes, it happens with startling regularity out there in the culture, but inside the safe and sacred confines of a church building, abortion has no place.

If only that were true.

CHAPTER 3
Child Sacrifice in Church

One of my coworkers was speaking with a Christian university campus minister about the prevalence of abortion at his school, and he dismissed the topic with a wave of his hand. "Abortion isn't prevalent at our school. Contraception is widely available, but our students also take sexual purity to heart."

I was suspicious of his answer, so I spoke with a recent graduate of that same university about her thoughts. "I suspect one in three women on campus have had an abortion," she said matter-of-factly. "It may be higher. Christian kids don't want to deal with the shame a pregnancy brings. So they abort instead of telling their parents."

More times than I can count, I've heard this remorseful comment from a Christian post-abortive parent: "I knew it was wrong to abort my child. I was brought up in the church and was pro-life. But I did it anyway."

But I did it anyway.

Why do Christians, many of whom profess to honor the sacredness of life, still abort their children? Why do they promote a pro-life worldview publicly but, when they face an unplanned pregnancy themselves, lose their conviction and take the life of their child? At

Online for Life, we have worked with thousands of families considering abortion. We often hear about clients' church attendance or religious beliefs, but those beliefs don't always seem to connect to the decision to abort. Oftentimes women will state that they know abortion is wrong or against their beliefs, but the circumstances overwhelm them. Here is one such note about a client from North Carolina: "Married—husband is pressuring for abortion b/c she is not working. Client says she is a Christian and knows abortion is wrong, but feeling the pressure."

At other times, a family simply isn't educated about abortion. They don't connect the dots between their faith and the taking of a human life. This is a story relayed to us by the nurse who met with a client and her boyfriend, as described in her notes:

> We started talking about abortion, the procedure, suction specifically since she is between 9-10 weeks pregnant. I explained it to her with the diagram. I also went over the immediate and long-term consequences of abortion. She was moved and said that she didn't want to make the wrong decision, that she needed her bf [boyfriend] to be inside. I asked her if her decision was based on how he reacted, and she said it wasn't, but she still wanted him to be there so he could hear everything I was explaining to her. I brought N [the boyfriend] in and explained it to him.
>
> Afterwards, he asked time alone to talk to Client. They talked for about 10 minutes, and she said that she needed to step outside but that she would be back. After about 15 minutes, she came back in and said that she had just come in to tell me that she couldn't go through

with it. I asked her to come back inside to talk. I asked her what happened and she said, "I just can't do this—it goes against everything I believe in. I was raised by Catholics and I'm a Christian. And I don't believe in this. Besides I know that I will fall back into drugs if I do this so I can forget. And I just can't do that to myself. I'm only 23 years old."

This client came to understand what abortion actually is through the nurse's counsel. She then related it to her Catholic upbringing while also comprehending the terrible consequence of abortion to her own emotional and spiritual health. She knew she would go back to a drug-based lifestyle just to numb the emotional pain of abortion.

There are women who feel so much pressure to abort that they reject their faith unless they encounter a friend, a support network, or a healthcare professional who will support them. Here's another client's story:

Client came to her first appointment very abortion-determined. She said this "must be" what she chooses, despite believing that it is wrong. Her husband supports her either way. She agreed to wait to come to the ultrasound. When she arrived for the ultrasound, she said that she had decided to keep the baby. When asked what made her decide, she said "coming here" to the center. She continued that the visit took her by surprise even though she had already made up her mind to abort. Later, when she talked to her husband, he said this was a sign from God.

This may be the most frequent scenario we see at Online for Life. The father of the child (in this case, the husband) doesn't support protecting the child. Note the father says he will "support" her either way, which is a neutral, insecure position. She feels a lack of security and makes a decision that she knows conflicts with her faith. Her faith, however, isn't enough to save the child unless she plugs into a caring network.

These are not isolated incidents.

Abortion is Rampant in Church

To equate child sacrifice with abortion is entirely fair and accurate, and abortion is occurring at alarmingly high rates within the church. I've culled information from the small number of recent studies on abortion and the church, and these numbers paint a picture that is essential to understanding the church's widespread silence.

I must stress that, although abortion affects all races, abortion in America disproportionately impacts the African-American community and church. Between 1973 and 2004, 30 percent of the African-American population was wiped out because of abortion. Black women are three times as likely to abort as other women.[90] This chapter focuses mainly on the rate of abortion occurrence and attitudes in the major Protestant and Catholic sects and isn't intended to focus on race. However, the abortion epidemic is so pervasive in the African-American church that I felt compelled to include a short section based on the work of two prominent African-American leaders at the end of this chapter.

Abortions in church communities are rampant. According to a study by the Guttmacher Institute, a pro-abortion research group:

Almost three-quarters of women obtaining abortions in 2008 reported a religious affiliation. The largest proportion was Protestant (37 percent), and most of the rest said that they were Catholic (28 percent) or that they had no religious affiliation (27 percent). One in five abortion patients identified themselves as born-again, evangelical, charismatic or fundamentalist; 75 percent of these were Protestant.[91]

Religious Affiliation of Women Obtaining Abortions, 2008

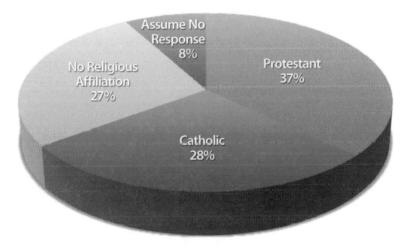

Enormous numbers of self-proclaimed Protestants and Catholics are taking the lives of their own children.

With approximately 1.2 million abortions in 2008, over 450,000 women who aborted claimed to be Protestant, with over 180,000 stating they were born-again, evangelical, or fundamentalist. Another 340,000 claimed to be Catholic. That means that over two-thirds of the women who aborted claimed a religious affiliation with a Protestant or Catholic church.[92] The remaining 7 percent who claimed a religious affiliation did not identify a specific religion.

Let that statistic sink in. Although to claim a religious affiliation and actually be a true believer in Jesus Christ can be two different things, the fact remains that most women who abort their children claim to be "religious" in some sense of the word.

Frequent or regular church attendance is apparently linked to a lower likelihood of abortion, as Guttmacher reported:

> In 2008, 15 percent of women having abortions reported attending religious services once a week or more, 13 percent attended one to three times a month and 32 percent attended less frequently; 41 percent never attended religious services. . . . Thus, tentative evidence suggests that women obtaining abortions attend religious services less frequently than all women.[93]

Church Attendance of Women Obtaining Abortions, 2008

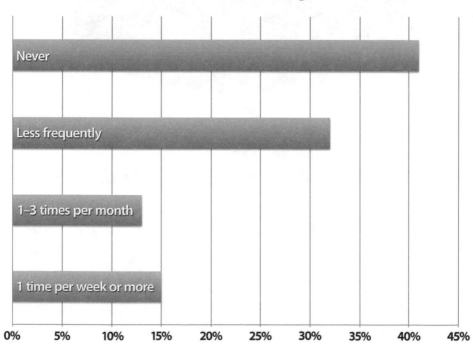

It's good news that church attendance appears to be a positive force for unborn children, but let's review a key point. If 15 percent of women who aborted attend a religious service once a week or more, another 13 percent attend one to three times a month, and another 32 percent attend at least once in a while, that means 60 percent of women who abort their children have at least some habit of attending church. In short, six out of ten women who abort claim to attend a church.

We may be tempted to think that these abortions only occur in churches that are pro-abortion or are doctrinally liberal. The National Association of Evangelicals, representing over forty-five thousand evangelical churches and forty denominations, reports:

> Eighty percent of unmarried evangelicals between the ages of eighteen and twenty nine have had sex. That's four out of five. Sixty-four percent have had sex within the last year. Unsurprisingly, there are natural consequences to ignoring God's good plan for sex. These single Christians are getting pregnant—30 percent of unmarried evangelicals have been pregnant or gotten someone pregnant.
>
> What may be the hardest fact to swallow is that many Christians are choosing to abort. Thirty-two percent of all unplanned pregnancies among evangelicals end in abortion.[94]

Think abortion isn't an issue in your church? Think again.

The Church Shrugs

Part of the reason so many churchgoers abort their children may be their church's nonchalance toward the abortion epidemic. It's an attitude shared by the public at large. Pew Research reports that a growing number of Americans regard abortion as not that consequential compared to other matters. Some 53 percent of Americans said in 2013 that abortion "is not that important compared to other issues," up from 48 percent in 2009 and 32 percent in 2006. Likewise, the percentage who think abortion is a "critical issue facing the country" fell from 28 percent in 2006 to 15 percent in 2009 and now rests at 18 percent.[95]

Pew's look at the church is fascinating and somewhat cryptic. Once again, regular church attendance is a key factor in how a person views the criticality of abortion. While 64 percent of churchgoers who attend weekly say abortion is a critical issue, just 33 percent of those who attend less often think abortion is important.

Likewise, religiously affiliated Americans are split on abortion. Some 60 percent of white evangelicals and Mormons want to see abortion criminalized in all or most cases. Jews and white mainline Protestants take the opposite view. Almost 90 percent of Jews and 63 percent of white mainline Protestants want abortion legal in all or most cases. Half of both black Protestants and white Catholics support legal abortion in all or most cases.[96]

Regular churchgoers may indicate abortion is a critical concern, but that doesn't mean they are unified about whether or not it is right or wrong. Pew reports that those who attend worship weekly or more frequently are split on whether or not abortion should be legal. While 50 percent of Americans who go to religious services at least weekly support overturning *Roe v. Wade*, 44 percent of weekly attenders do not want *Roe* thrown out.[97]

That the church is not aggressively and agonizingly concerned about abortion should be of great concern to all of us. As John Paul II said, "[N]ot only is the fact of the destruction of so many human lives still to be born or in their final stage extremely grave and disturbing, but no less grave and disturbing is the fact that conscience itself, darkened as it were by such widespread conditioning, is finding it increasingly difficult to distinguish between good and evil in what concerns the basic value of human life."[98]

Morality and the Law

Pew dug deeper into the tendencies of the church as it related to *Roe v. Wade*:

> There continue to be substantial religious and partisan differences over whether to overturn *Roe v. Wade* and over the broader question of whether abortion should be legal or illegal in all or most cases.
>
> White evangelical Protestants are the only major religious group in which a majority (54 percent) favors completely overturning the *Roe v. Wade* decision. Large percentages of white mainline Protestants (76 percent), black Protestants (65 percent) and white Catholics (63 percent) say the ruling should not be overturned. Fully 82 percent of the religiously unaffiliated oppose overturning *Roe v. Wade*.[99]

It's essential to extract a key point from this study. Asking whether *Roe* should be overturned is a way of determining the strength of a person's life-affirming convictions. If someone wants *Roe* dismissed, we can assume that person understands abortion is the unjust killing of a human being and should be illegal. If someone doesn't want to see *Roe* overturned, we assume he or she considers abortion to be appropriate in at least some circumstances. White evangelical Protestants favor the end of *Roe* by only the slimmest of margins. It's staggering that 63 percent of Catholics (who follow the Vatican, the staunchest of pro-life religious groups) say *Roe* shouldn't be overturned.

It is possible that some of the church's reluctance to return to a nation that protects unborn life and outlaws abortion is attributed to the general level of ignorance about *Roe v. Wade* and *Doe v. Bolton*. Many people don't understand that these two rulings provide for abortion-on-demand at any stage of pregnancy. Yet even if most don't comprehend the tremendous permissiveness of the rule laid down by the court, the results also suggest that large groups of American Christians want abortion to be legal—at least for some people in certain circumstances.

Another conundrum is the various groups' answers to questions about the moral acceptability of abortion. While 73 percent of white evangelicals said abortion is morally wrong, only 54 percent said *Roe* should be overturned. Apparently 20 percent of the white evangelical church thinks abortion is wrong but should still be legal. This irony may exist because of an erroneous but popular cultural assumption that "we shouldn't legislate morality." This assumption undergirds many of the pro-abortion arguments, namely the "I can do whatever I want with my body" mantra or the "Get your religion out of my uterus" cries of modern-day liberal feminists.

"We shouldn't legislate morality" is so commonly accepted in some circles that we don't always stop and think about the foolishness of this claim. The primary purpose of laws is to legislate morality. Murder is illegal because murder is wrong. There are laws to protect us from being murdered and to punish those who do so. "Murder is wrong" is a moral claim; therefore the law exists to enforce it. Laws exist to promote and enforce morality, whether that involves theft, rape, violence, discrimination, or a host of other wrongs. If abortion is morally wrong, abortion should be illegal. To say abortion is morally wrong but should still be legal is inconsistent and illogical.

Also surprising are the decent-sized segments in each group who think abortion isn't a moral issue at all:

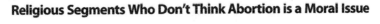

Religious Segments Who Don't Think Abortion is a Moral Issue

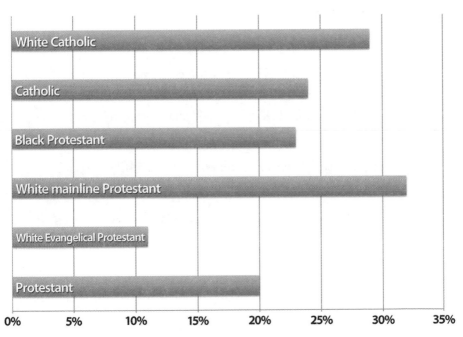

Almost one-quarter of Catholics don't think abortion is a moral issue, while one-fifth of Protestants feel the same. Fully one-third of white mainline churchgoers don't see abortion as a moral issue. These are minority groups to be sure, but these are significant numbers. If you are a white Catholic, one in three adults in your parish doesn't think abortion is a moral issue. If you are a Presbyterian, the same results apply. One-third of your congregation doesn't see the connection between killing an unborn child and morality.

While the Protestant Church appears to be confused on the biblical, moral, and legal framework of abortion, the American Catholic Church seems to be at odds with its own teachings. In a 2005 Gallup poll of Catholics, 875 self-described Catholics were asked how important church teaching on abortion was to them. The results suggest that many take an à la carte approach to Catholicism on the issue of abortion:

- Very important   43.8%
- Somewhat important   32.6%
- Not important at all   22.9%

In addition, 58 percent of Catholics said a person can be a good Catholic without obeying the church hierarchy's teaching on abortion.[100]

So while over 75 percent of respondents said the Vatican's teachings about abortion were at least somewhat important, about 60 percent said they would still be in good standing if they ignored the teachings.

These respondents should consider reading Pope John Paul's *Evangelium Vitae* (Gospel of Life), published in 1995, which may be the most elegant, comprehensive look at the sacredness of human life and the church's commitment to protecting it. We would all do well to digest its teachings and then determine whether or not we have the option to ignore it.

Conditional Abortions

One more study shows further evidence of the confusion within the church on abortion. The US Congregational Life Survey in 2001 questioned 1,106 church attendees and asked under what conditions abortion should be legal. The majority of churchgoers responded that it should be legal if the mother's life is in danger. In the case of rape, the following groups said it should be legal:

- 48% Catholics
- 73% Mainline Protestant
- 34% Conservative Protestant

If the baby is mentally impaired:

- 18% Catholics
- 40% Mainline Protestant
- 8% Conservative Protestant

If the woman or family can't afford the child:

- 7% Catholic
- 22% Mainline Protestant
- 4% Conservative Protestant

If the woman doesn't want the child:

- 10% Catholic
- 25% Mainline Protestant
- 5% Conservative Protestant[101]

Mainline Protestants lead the way on permitting abortions under circumstances other than protecting the life of the mother. It is interesting to note that, in all groups, the church considers the mother's unwillingness to have the child to be a better reason to abort than financial challenges.

The "pro-choice" marketing plan over the past forty years has indeed been effective.

Reasons for Silence

It's fair to conclude that abortion remains a divisive, confusing topic in American churches and one that, in many cases, is treated with silence. We shouldn't be surprised, therefore, that the incidence of abortion inside the church is so high. Silence combined with confusion is a bad recipe for the unborn children of our nation.

The question is, why? Why is there so much confusion, ignorance, and indecision in the church about the killing of innocent lives?

A simple answer may be that abortion is rarely discussed or taught by church leaders. People are not informed about the scriptural, moral, ethical, and social ramifications of abortion. We receive very little factual information from the media. If our churches ignore it as well, where are we to get truthful, relevant teaching?

Why don't churches talk about it? There are numerous factors, but here are some of the top reasons:

1. "We only preach using an expositional method."

"Expositional teaching" is a theological term that means teaching what the Scripture plainly says, usually in a linear fashion. It is typically contrasted with "topical teaching," which is teaching about a topic using various scriptures as support. For example, a pastor or priest who is teaching through John 1, verse by verse, is teaching expositionally. A pastor or priest who is teaching about marriage and using various passages from the Bible is teaching topically. Expositional teachers tend to steer clear of topical preaching because they fear that they might pull a passage out of context to make a point supporting a topical assertion. By teaching what the Bible plainly says and staying focused on a particular passage, the expositional teacher remains true to the text as it is without potentially falling into interpretive errors.

I'm not advocating for one or the other, and they aren't necessarily opposites. As Pastor Geoff Ashley reminded me, "Expositional preaching is more technically concerned not with going verse by verse, but by drawing out the meaning of the text. All preaching should be expositional even if it is topical." I've heard marvelous messages using both approaches, and I've heard poor sermons from both as well.

I think that some expositional teachers, however, avoid mention of contemporary issues, news, or items not explicitly mentioned in the Bible. Because the word "abortion" doesn't appear in Scripture, it isn't a part of their preaching philosophy. As we'll discover, however, the Bible is abundantly clear on abortion, even though the word itself doesn't appear. Part of the role of a teacher is to apply his or her teachings to the current time and place. In an effort to "stay true to Scripture" using expositional teaching, I fear some preachers have lost relevancy to our culture. We are to be salt and light, and thus we must be willing to apply Scripture, regardless of our preaching philosophy, to current and pressing topics.

2. "Abortion is a political issue."

Many church leaders don't want to address what they believe is a political issue. To do so might put their nonprofit status at risk or offend churchgoers. The truth is that to politicize abortion is to mischaracterize and minimize it. Abortion is primarily a spiritual issue, and as such, the church is required to deal with it.

3. "We believe abortion should be permissible."

Of course there are numerous churches that are pro-abortion. If church leadership supports the abortion practice, it is understandable why abortion would be prevalent in that denomination or specific location.

4. "I'm hiding something."

Near the end of 2013, a life-affirming pregnancy center in the South saw a woman in her thirties who was strongly considering abortion. The woman shared her story about how she couldn't have a baby because she owned a business that was in financial trouble. Financial insecurity is a very common reason women say they are considering abortion, so the pregnancy center reached out to some friends who offered to help the young mother with her difficult situation. However, as the woman continued to share her story over the next few days, the counselor realized her finances weren't the only issue. The father (the couple wasn't married) wanted her to abort the child and was pressuring her to do so.

The reason he wanted her to abort? He was a pastor and didn't want to be embarrassed in front of his congregation. He wanted to kill his child to cover his indiscretion.

Abortion and the Black Church

Rev. Dean Nelson, chairman of the Frederick Douglass Foundation and one of the nation's leading African-American pro-life voices, believes abortion in the black church is exponentially widespread. Though it's been reported that African-American women make up some 14 percent of all American females, over 30 percent of all abortions in our country are carried out on black women.

Nelson believes about half of congregants in black churches have had an abortion or have been party to one. He also maintains that a large number of black church leaders have had abortions in their past. This, coupled with the politicization of abortion in the black community, leads to widespread silence in the African-American church. There are most certainly exceptions to this silence, and

Nelson has worked aggressively within black church leadership to raise awareness about abortion in an effort to stem the tide of death.[102]

If pastors, priests, elders, deacons, and lay leaders have aborted children, they put themselves at great risk if they encourage abortion to be discussed and taught in church. Even if they have sought and found forgiveness, they fear the potential backlash if they confess that sin to their parish or congregation. Or, in the case of the young pastor mentioned previously as "hiding something," they refuse to teach against something they are participating in, even if killing a child is their way of covering up their own indiscretion.

In 2011, black pro-life leader Walter Hoye wrote a series of articles called "Betrayal Trauma." Hoye quotes Dennis Howard, the founder and president of the Movement for a Better America, on the abortion epidemic inside the black community:

> Let's be honest. Even slavery—as awful as it was—pales in comparison to the evil of abortion. At its peak, slavery affected the lives of perhaps three million Blacks. We have already ended the lives of six times that many Blacks in [less than] four decades of abortion, and eighteen times that many unborn children of all races and colors.

Hoye then notes that it took the Ku Klux Klan eighty-six years (from 1882–1968) to lynch 3,446 blacks. "At the current rate Black Americans are aborting their children, in less than four days, more Black Americans will be killed by abortion than have been killed by the Ku Klux Klan in its entire history."

Despite the systematic elimination of blacks in America due to abortion, Hoye believes most black leaders remain passively silent for four primary reasons:

1. Black leadership rejects the pro-life effort because he or she is post-abortive.

2. Some black leaders are racist and don't wish to engage in a pro-life movement that is predominantly led by white leaders.

3. Some black leaders are compromised. If a black church leader is ministering to a congregation that consists of a majority of post-abortive men and women, preaching and teaching on abortion could split his church and ruin his ministry.

4. Black leadership is often uninformed about the number and impact of abortions on the black community.[103]

Whether because of silence, personal abortion histories, racism, confusion, ignorance, bad doctrine, or shame, many American churches sit idly by while the killing continues. Beneath all of these reasons, however, there lies one incontrovertible fact. When a church is passively silent about abortion, they are actively affirming what the media has proclaimed and what the culture believes: the unborn child is less valuable than the rest of us.

PART 2
Abortion and the Bible

CHAPTER 4
Is God the Author of All Life?

Imagine walking up to a playground full of kindergartners. There are thirty-five of them laughing, playing, throwing balls, and enjoying a beautiful spring day. These children come from a variety of backgrounds, family situations, and races. No two children are exactly the same, of course, and this group has tremendous diversity. Some even come from very difficult circumstances. One child was conceived in rape. Another child's parents couldn't afford him. Yet another child was born out of adultery. But most of the kids come from good homes, and most look like they are strong, healthy, and well behaved. None of them is perfect, of course. A few have allergies, and one or two have ADHD. There are a few children who are perpetually misbehaving. Some have more challenging situations, and one has Down syndrome. Yet they all share a common bond: they are all five years old, and they are all innocently playing together during recess.

Then something unspeakable happens. All thirty-five children are killed. They are not shot, nor do they die of a disease. They don't die in a tragic accident. They are drawn and quartered. Their limbs are ripped from their bodies. They are decapitated in the most brutal, horrific fashion imaginable. The devastation, gore, loss of life, and horror causes you to be ill, and you break down weeping in front of the playground, unable to speak or describe what you've just witnessed.

Now imagine that this awful scene is played out on more than one playground. Thirty-five kindergarten children are killed on a second playground in another city. Then it happens again, and again, and again. On one hundred playgrounds across America, thirty-five children lose their lives through dismemberment. Thirty-five hundred five-year-olds killed in the space of just one day, for doing nothing more than playing innocently on playgrounds. Then it happens again tomorrow, and the next day, and the next.

If this immeasurable tragedy started happening in America today, would the American church rise up to stop the killing? Would pastors preach about it in their pulpits? Would they search and apply the Word of God, encouraging and provoking their congregations to be actively, tangibly involved in protecting these little children? I suspect many churches in America, if not all, would drop whatever they were doing and run to help these victims.

But what if we lived in some twisted, corrupt version of America where this daily killing of 3,500 children was legal? The government, for reasons such as population control, social manipulation, or racism, sanctioned the killing of kindergartners in this brutal fashion. Would the American church still run to protect innocent children from being ripped limb from limb? Or would they say that it was a political issue, and that the church was separate from the state?

Perhaps some churches would avoid entering the conflict if the killing was legal. But it is likely many churches would still aggressively, passionately, and vocally work to protect and defend the lives of the kindergartners, even if doing so meant they were in conflict with the government and faced persecution, imprisonment, or worse.

And here is the difficult follow-up question that we must answer with candor and transparency: What is the moral, scriptural difference between a five-year-old kindergarten child and a baby in the womb? We must also ask: Why is the American church not rising up aggressively, passionately, and vocally to protect and defend the thirty-five-hundred children who are destroyed every day inside their mothers' bellies? Why do many American churches stay silent, citing abortion as a political is-sue, not a spiritual one? Why do they avoid preaching or teaching about it, instead expressing concern about privacy issues and the "personal" nature of an abortion decision?

Though the responses to those questions are numerous, there is one answer that undergirds them all, and it is incontrovertible. It is painfully obvious why the American church is, on the whole, silent on abortion. It does not understand or believe that an unborn life has the same value as a life already born.

I strongly suspect that the church would rise up and do whatever it took to prevent the deaths of thirty-five-hundred kindergarten children every day in our country. Even if the killings were legal and sanctioned by the government, most churches would still work with great fervor to stop the killings.

When we speak of the unborn, however, I can already hear the "buts" starting to echo from various corners of the country:

- "But the unborn child may have a birth defect."
- "But the unborn child may grow up in a destitute home."
- "But the unborn child may not be wanted."
- "But the unborn child may be the result of rape or incest."
- "But the unborn child is not protected by our government."
- "But the mother's rights are greater than the unborn child's rights."
- "But the unborn child may not feel pain."

Now replace the word "unborn child" with "kindergarten child" in each of the sentences above. Take a moment and re-read the statements with that substitution.

Were you horrified at the thought of killing a kindergarten child because she is poor, has a birth defect, or is unwanted by her parents? Did you have a stronger reaction when you thought about a kindergarten child being killed than you did a pre-born child? If so, you are among the millions of people who devalue life in the womb.

If we call ourselves Christians, however, and claim to follow God, then we must ask ourselves whether or not God views life the same way. Does He consider life in the womb to be of less value and less worthy of protection than the kindergarten child?

There has been a small amount of work done over the past forty years by theologians, preachers, and teachers on the subject of God and life in the womb. But compared to topics such as marriage, pornography, discipleship, prayer, church-planting, missions, and the family, abortion barely shows up as a blip on the radar. Take a stroll around your local Christian bookstore and see how many texts you can find on the subject. Good luck finding one or two.

This is staggering considering the fifty-six million dead Americans at the hands of abortion. The greatest holocaust in American history barely gets mentioned in bookstores dedicated to Christian living.

I believe the Bible provides a clear, logical, and defensible argument related to the sanctity of all human life, and that includes life in the womb. As I pored over the Scriptures and other abortion-related works while doing research for this book, I was struck by how clearly the Bible speaks to this issue. And I began to see a simple, three-step argument emerge that I hope revolutionizes the way Christians think about God, abortion, and the church. As with any issue we wrestle with, the Bible provides clarity and instruction.

I'm proposing this easy, three-step apologetic defense based on the following questions, and we will look at each one in turn.

1. Is God the author of all human life?

Is God the author of each and every human being? Is every child an image-bearer of God? Is there such a thing as an unplanned pregnancy to God? Or does God have a unique purpose and plan for every person, regardless of how or why he or she is conceived?

2. Does God give man the right to kill innocent human life?

If God does create every person, does the Creator give people the right to kill innocent humans? And, very importantly, does He give us that right at some stages but not others? Is life less valuable before birth and, therefore, allowed to be terminated?

3. Is the Church commanded to protect and defend innocent human life?

If we conclude that God is the author of every life and God does not permit us to destroy His innocent human creations, then the last question addresses our response. Does God expressly command His followers to protect and preserve His innocent human creations?

Is God the Author of All Life?

If you answered yes, then you must be able to address the vast number of unplanned pregnancies in America, even when conception occurs through a sinful act (e.g., rape, incest, and adultery). If you answered no, then you need to be prepared to confront whether God is responsible for any lives at all.

We'll answer the question by exploring the following:

1. Is God in control?
2. Does God create babies that are "unplanned" or "unwanted"?
3. Is a baby always "good"?

The Sovereignty of God

Unlike the small number of books written by Christians about abortion, there is no shortage of texts written about the sovereignty of God. A brief search for "God's sovereignty" at Amazon.com yields over eighteen thousand works, and I doubt that scratches the surface of all that has been written over the centuries.

Let's take a brief look at what others have written about God's sovereignty and then apply it to the topic of abortion and unborn life.

Webster's Dictionary defines "sovereignty" as "possessed of supreme power" or "unlimited in extent."[104]

The Bible teaches that God is the ultimate, sovereign ruler of the entire universe. As popular scholar R. C. Sproul has said, "There is no maverick molecule if God is sovereign."[105]

Holman's *Illustrated Bible Dictionary* defines God's sovereignty as

> [the] biblical teaching that God possesses all power and is the ruler of all things (Ps. 135:6; Dan. 4:34–35). God rules and works according to His eternal purpose, even through events that seem to contradict or oppose His rule.[106]

It's important to note that God is sovereign even though life sometimes seems out of control, unfair, or downright unjust. As we'll explore below, God is sovereign over life even when life is created through tragedy, hardship, crime, or challenging circumstances.

Both Testaments are filled with references to God's sovereignty. A brief survey of the Old Testament shows a constant theme—God is in complete control of all things, even when things appear out of control.

The Psalmist speaks about the power and majesty of God when he writes in Psalm 103:

> The LORD has established His throne in the heavens,
> And His sovereignty rules over all. (Ps. 103:19)

Psalm 135 declares:

> Whatever the LORD pleases, He does,
> In heaven and in earth, in the seas and in all deeps.
> (Ps. 135:6)

Isaiah reminds his readers in chapter 46:9–10:

> Remember the former things long past,
> For I am God, and there is no other;
> I am God, and there is no one like Me,
> Declaring the end from the beginning,
> And from ancient times things which have not been done,
> Saying, "My purpose will be established,
> And I will accomplish all My good pleasure."

When Nebuchadnezzar returned to his senses after a period of divinely-ordained madness, he recognized God for who He is:

> For His dominion is an everlasting dominion,
> And His kingdom endures from generation to generation.
> All the inhabitants of the earth are accounted as nothing,
> But He does according to His will in the host of heaven
> And among the inhabitants of earth;
> And no one can ward off His hand
> Or say to Him, "What have You done?" (Dan. 4:34–35)

Perhaps the Old Testament poster child for discovering anew the sovereignty of God is Job, who suffered greatly yet remained faithful:

> But He is unique and who can turn Him?
> And what His soul desires, that He does. (Job 23:13)

While the Bible talks about God's sovereignty over all things in relation to kingdoms, rulers, and the universe, it also makes clear God is divinely involved with the smallest of details. For example:

> O LORD, You have searched me and known me.
> You know when I sit down and when I rise up;
> You understand my thought from afar.
> You scrutinize my path and my lying down,
> And are intimately acquainted with all my ways.
> Even before there is a word on my tongue,
> Behold, O LORD, You know it all. (Ps. 139:1–4)

Likewise, we see in Matthew:

> Are not two sparrows sold for a cent? And yet not one
> of them will fall to the ground apart from your Father.
> But the very hairs of your head are all numbered.
> So do not fear; you are more valuable than many
> sparrows. (Matt. 10:29–31)

Whether the fate of nations, the movement of winds on the earth, or the number of hairs on our head, there is nothing outside of God's control, knowledge, and plan.

The Sovereignty of God and Creation

Holman's dictionary elaborates further on the sovereignty of God:

> Scripture emphasizes God's rule in three areas: creation, human history, and redemption. Scripture testifies clearly to God's rule over His creation (Gen. 1; Mark 4:35–41; Rom. 8:20–21), including Christ's sustaining and governing of all things (Heb. 1:3, Col. 1:15–17). The Bible affirms also that God rules human history according to His purpose, from ordinary events in the lives of individuals (Judg. 14:1–4; Prov. 16:9, 33) to the rise, affairs, and fall of nations (Ps. 22:28; Hab. 1:6; Acts 17:26). Scripture depicts redemption as the work of God alone. God, according to His eternal purpose, takes the initiative in the provision and application of salvation and in enabling man's willing acceptance (John 17:2; Rom. 8:29–30; Eph. 1:3–14; 2 Thess. 2:13–14; 2 Tim. 1:9–10).[107]

Holman's description of God's sovereignty in three key areas—creation, human history, and redemption—is compelling. Because we are discussing created human beings, it is worth diving a bit deeper into what God's sovereignty over creation means.

Psalm 24:1 says,

> The earth is the Lord's, and all it contains,
> The world, and those who dwell in it.[108]

The psalmist makes clear that the entire world belongs to God. The phrase "and those who dwell" relates to all of earth's inhabitants. Not only do all people—past, present, and future—belong to God, but He is personally and intimately involved in our very creation and existence.

Psalm 139 is often quoted as the quintessential pro-life chapter, filled with wonder and rich with meaning. While some scholars dismiss it as poetry and not a definitive statement on embryology or science, it is a powerful passage worth exploring for its statements about God.

Unlike modern English, where the most important part of the story is usually the end, ancient literature was often constructed in a way that emphasized the middle of a passage. If you imagine a bell curve, you'll note that the curve starts and ends at the bottom, while the peak of the curve is right in the middle. Psalm 139 is constructed in such a way.

David, the writer of the psalm, starts with a declaration that God has "searched" him and knows him fully. The original Hebrew word has a sense of considering in detail, analyzing, or exploring. God knows David better than David does.

In fact, the first six verses outline God's omniscience, His knowledge of all things:

O Lord, You have searched me and known me.

You know when I sit down and when I rise up;

You understand my thought from afar.

You scrutinize my path and my lying down,

And are intimately acquainted with all my ways.

Even before there is a word on my tongue,

Behold, O Lord, You know it all.

You have enclosed me behind and before,

And laid Your hand upon me.

Such knowledge is too wonderful for me;

It is too high, I cannot attain to it.

David then proclaims that God is omnipresent—He exists everywhere. There is no night to God, there is nowhere in the universe hidden from Him:

Where can I go from Your Spirit?

Or where can I flee from Your presence?

If I ascend to heaven, You are there;

If I make my bed in Sheol, behold, You are there.

If I take the wings of the dawn,

If I dwell in the remotest part of the sea,

Even there Your hand will lead me,

And Your right hand will lay hold of me.

If I say, "Surely the darkness will overwhelm me,

And the light around me will be night,"

Even the darkness is not dark to You,

And the night is as bright as the day.

Darkness and light are alike to You.

God is omniscient and omnipresent, but He is also omnipotent, or all-powerful. David describes this through the act of God creating David himself:

> For You formed my inward parts;
> You wove me in my mother's womb.
> I will give thanks to You, for I am fearfully and won-
> derfully made;
> Wonderful are Your works,
> And my soul knows it very well.
> My frame was not hidden from You,
> When I was made in secret,
> And skillfully wrought in the depths of the earth;
> Your eyes have seen my unformed substance;
> And in Your book were all written
> The days that were ordained for me,
> When as yet there was not one of them.
> How precious also are Your thoughts to me, O God!
> How vast is the sum of them!
> If I should count them, they would outnumber the
> sand.
> When I awake, I am still with You.[109]

God has power over all creation, He is responsible for the origin of every human life, He ordains all of our days, and His ways are infinitely beyond our ability to grasp or understand.

In a fashion somewhat typical of David, he responds to God's greatness with a proclamation of loyalty:

O that You would slay the wicked, O God;

Depart from me, therefore, men of bloodshed.

For they speak against You wickedly,

And Your enemies take Your name in vain.

Do I not hate those who hate You, O LORD?

And do I not loathe those who rise up against You?

I hate them with the utmost hatred;

They have become my enemies.[110]

David closes the psalm in the same way he started—asking God to "search" him, relying on God to know him more intimately and work out any sin or harm:

Search me, O God, and know my heart;

Try me and know my anxious thoughts;

And see if there be any hurtful way in me,

And lead me in the everlasting way.

Note the "bell curve." David starts and ends with the request and knowledge that God searches him. He begins and ends with the same thought—God knows him intimately, completely, and wholly.

Why does God have such an amazing knowledge of David, his thoughts, his mind, and his heart? *Because God created David.* Consider again the middle, or high point, of the psalm:

For You formed my inward parts;

You wove me in my mother's womb.

I will give thanks to You, for I am fearfully and wonderfully made;

Wonderful are Your works,

And my soul knows it very well.[111]

Amidst a beautifully orchestrated description of God's omniscience, omnipresence, and omnipotence, the centerpiece is the wonderment at how God is the Author of Life, carefully "weaving" us together in our mother's womb. David highlights the act of creation of human beings and stops to exclaim how amazing that is. God knows David better than David does because God created him.

Job, when responding to one of his not-so-helpful friends, acknowledges God as his creator. He also recognizes God has control of joys and sorrows, health and pain:

Your hands fashioned and made me altogether,

And would You destroy me?

Remember now, that You have made me as clay;

And would You turn me into dust again?

Did You not pour me out like milk

And curdle me like cheese;

Clothe me with skin and flesh,

And knit me together with bones and sinews?

You have granted me life and lovingkindness;

And Your care has preserved my spirit.[112]

God is in complete control of the universe and intimately involved with every detail of our individual lives. He is the creator of everything, including all human life. He knows each one of us intimately, completely, and wholly because He made each of us.

Never Unplanned, Never Unwanted

If we accept this truth, that God knows each of us completely because He created each of us, then we also conclude the following: in the mind and will of God, there is no such thing as an unplanned or unwanted pregnancy.

In light of our brief look at His sovereignty, how could it be otherwise? Is God surprised when a baby is "unexpectedly" conceived? Is He wringing His hands when a woman realizes she is pregnant and the pregnancy is "unplanned"? If we stop to think about it, the thought is absurd. God, who created billions of stars, planets, and galaxies, also created Earth. Not only did He create Earth, He created everything inside, on, and over the Earth.

He created sex. He invented it to be within the confines of marriage, and one of its primary purposes is procreation. Despite massive advancements in embryology and fetology, we still haven't figured out exactly how new human life springs into existence. We know the egg and sperm get together, and we know a lot about human development. But no one has figured out exactly what happens when that egg and sperm join. How do two cells from two different people suddenly change into an entirely new being with unique chromosomes and self-initiate the growth process into increasingly greater stages of maturity? How and when does a soul enter a body?

New life remains a mystery and a miracle.

If God knows the number of hairs on our head, and if He knows when a sparrow falls, is He taken by surprise by new life? Did He knit David together in his mother's womb, but not knit everyone else? Does He create some people but not others?

If we say that God is surprised by an unplanned pregnancy, then it means that God isn't sovereign. God is either in complete control, or

He isn't in control at all. He is either the author of all life or the author of none.

There are Christians who believe God is personally involved with the creation of each human life. There are others who believe God created Adam and Eve with the ability to reproduce, and reproduction occurs through natural means originally ordained by God. Though I tend toward the latter, it doesn't diminish my point. If God is sovereign, every human life, whether directly created by God or created through the process He invented, is an image-bearer of the Creator and is part of His divine plan.

God's Creation is Good

What God creates is good.

The creation account in Genesis 1 proves that point. God creates the heavens and the earth, the stars, the sun, the moon, the oceans, plants, and animals. After each day of creation, He pronounces His creation good. On the sixth day He creates humans. Then He pronounces all of creation (including humans) "very good" (Gen. 1:31).

In our American culture, we've come to believe that unplanned pregnancies are a universal negative. In some churches, we equate the sin of sex outside of marriage with the actual pregnancy. Unmarried sex is sinful and bad, so the pregnancy and child must be bad.

How quickly we dismiss the fact that God works through our sin, mistakes, "accidents," screw-ups, and poor decisions for our good and His glory. We are all born in and corrupted by sin, but God uses even our corrupted nature to accomplish His will.

Perhaps we should remind ourselves how God used a murderer, Moses, to lead His people out of Egypt. Or how God used a some-time-spineless man like Abraham to become the father of many nations.

Or how God used a prostitute named Rahab to save the lives of Israelite spies. Or how a last-in-line, ruddy shepherd named David became the king of Israel. Despite being an adulterer and murderer (to cover up an unplanned pregnancy), David is still known as a man after God's own heart. Or how Saul, a killer of Christians, became the apostle Paul and wrote a majority of the New Testament.

God uses messed-up people and their sins for good all the time. In fact, a cursory reading of Scripture leads me to believe God loves taking our mistakes and turning them into beauty, just so we can marvel at the greatness of the God we serve.

Does this mean we should increase our sin so God can do His work? Of course not. As Paul reminds us in Romans 6:1–2:

> What shall we say then? Are we to continue in sin so that grace may increase?
> May it never be! How shall we who died to sin still live in it?

I am not at all justifying the rampant, sex-saturated culture we live in or the plague of unmarried sex that is destroying our homes and families. I am saying that God is at work through those sins, and a new human being is an act of beautiful, marvelous, miraculous, mind-blowing creation. And if a child is conceived in sin, she herself is not the sin, but beauty from ashes.

This is a critical distinction for Christians. In some churches, women abort because they fear the shame and embarrassment of unveiling their unplanned pregnancy. They view their pregnancy and unborn child as a permanent reminder of their sin and don't want to be exposed. And unfortunately, in some churches, their fears are well-founded.

Some congregations refuse to throw baby showers for unwed mothers because they don't want to "encourage inappropriate behavior." Unwed mothers are genuinely shunned because of their indiscretions. This type of legalism is deadly to the mother and child.

Adultery and sex outside of marriage are sin; that is biblical fact. Hebrews 13:4 reads, "Let marriage be held in honor among all, and let the marriage bed be undefiled, for God will judge the sexually immoral and adulterous." Romans 13:3 states, "Let us walk properly as in the daytime, not in orgies and drunkenness, not in sexual immorality and sensuality, not in quarreling and jealousy."

We must be relentless, however, in our displays of repentance, forgiveness, and grace to those facing unplanned pregnancies. To somehow characterize their sexual sin as worse as or more shameful than our own sin is arrogant and blind.

And a baby, regardless of how it was conceived, is a precious gift of God. A baby is always a special, miraculous human capable of amazing things. Each baby is a living, breathing work of art, created by an infinitely creative God. A baby is always good. I don't mean "good" in the theological sense of perfect or sinless, because we are all conceived in and marred by sin. New life is "good" as in a blessing, a wonderful act of creation, or a special benefit to our lives.

Have you ever created something beautiful? Of course you have. It may have been a poem, a piece of music, or a sculpture. It may have been a business plan, a financial solution, or a winning strategy. Perhaps it was a fashion design, a delicious meal, or a wonderfully fattening dessert. We've all created something beautiful. How would you feel if someone destroyed your creation? What if someone threw your painting in the fire? Or deleted your business plan? What if someone tore your dessert to pieces? Would you be upset, sad, or angry?

Each human being is infinitely more complex, beautiful, and precious than anything you or I could create. How grieved is our Creator when we tear His creation to pieces?

Made in the Image of God

It is beyond amazing that no two human beings are the same. There are currently some seven billion people on the planet, and every one of them is utterly unique. No one living right now is a copy of anyone who ever lived, is living now, or will be born in the future.

Billions of people have and will inhabit the earth, and each one is singularly unique. Why? Because God is an infinitely creative God. Even in our diversity, God shows us His creative genius. Each person, whether planned or not, is a masterpiece of a majestic God. Not only is each of us created uniquely, but we each have a unique purpose. We each come hardwired with gifts, talents, and skills.

It is impossible to calculate the impact of fifty six million lost human beings, each with a special purpose, over the last four decades. How many skilled craftsmen, athletes, businesswomen, artisans, teachers, surgeons, and soldiers have we killed in the womb? How many mothers, fathers, sisters, and brothers? How many best friends, counselors, comforters, and—yes—pastors and priests have we lost to abortion?

In a culture that increasingly devalues and demeans human beings, we tend to forget just how special we are. We save the whales but abort our children. We get excited about the possibility of a single-celled organism on Mars, but we refuse to acknowledge the value of life in the womb. If you destroy a bald eagle egg, you may be fined up to $250,000. But a woman can destroy her own child for $400.

How can we know that each and every human being, regardless of the circumstances of conception, is infinitely valuable, unique, and created with purpose? Because unlike every other created thing in the universe, we are made in the image of God. This fact is the cornerstone and bedrock argument for proving that God is the author of all life. We are uniquely created and endowed with abilities and characteristics that no other creature on earth possesses. Unlike every other created thing, we were created to have a personal, intimate relationship with our Creator.

Genesis 1:26–27 says:

> Then God said, "Let Us make man in Our image, according to Our likeness; and let them rule over the fish of the sea and over the birds of the sky and over the cattle and over all the earth, and over every creeping thing that creeps on the earth."
>
> God created man in His own image, in the image of God He created him; male and female He created them.

Though humans are certainly not divine, we are made in the image of God. We have some common characteristics with God such as a personality, the capacity to love, the ability to make decisions, etc. We are the only created thing on earth that has this honor—the Imago Dei.

Secondly, because we are created in God's image as relational beings, we have the capability to have a personal, real relationship with Him through Jesus Christ. We relate to Him and, miraculously, He relates to us. John Paul II expounded on this point in his *Evangelium Vitae* (Gospel of Life):

> When he presents the heart of his redemptive mission, Jesus says, "I came that they may have life, and have it

abundantly" (John 10:10) . . . It is precisely in this "life" that all the aspects and stages of human life achieve their full significance.[113]

The entire Bible, from Genesis to Revelation, is a love story. It is a story of a loving God who created us, not because He needed someone to love, but to freely give love. It is a story of a breach in that loving relationship when mankind fell into sin, and it is a story of a God who gave Himself so that our relationship with Him could be restored. We are the only created beings with the potential for this relationship. Jesus didn't die for whales, eagles, or rose blossoms. He died for human beings, and it is us He calls friends.

God is the author of all life. Each human being, regardless of how he or she is conceived, has priceless value, uniqueness, and purpose.

CHAPTER 5
Does God Give Man the Right to Kill Innocent Life?

Erin was freaking out. She knew she shouldn't have slept with him. But he had wanted to have sex with her, and he had not-so-subtly implied that their relationship would be at an impasse if they didn't move to the next level. Erin liked him, even thought she loved him. Jake was funny, athletic, and charming. They had been seeing each other for a few weeks and, when you are in college, that's like dating for years.

Six weeks after their night together, she knew she was in trouble. The lines on the Walgreens pregnancy test confirmed it. Her parents were going to kill her. They wouldn't kill her for having sex. Growing up in their mainline Protestant church, sex was one of those things her parents rarely discussed. But everyone assumed everyone, whether married or not, was doing it.

Her parents would kill her for not being careful.

She immediately decided not to tell them. She wouldn't tell Jake, either. She wasn't sure how he would respond, but she suspected he would want her to get it taken care of. Besides, as a sophomore in college, how would he provide for a baby, even if he wanted it? No, Erin would end the pregnancy, and no one would be the wiser. Her parents would never know. And Jake, even if he did find out, would be grateful for her prompt action.

When Erin searched for an abortion provider online, she found plenty of clinics in her area, but there was also a listing for a pregnancy center. She didn't know what a pregnancy center was, but since she was pregnant, she gave them a call. They asked her to come in for a free ultrasound to make sure the pregnancy was viable, and she agreed. Her ensuing conversation with the counselor at the center reveals the mindset of many Christians today:

Counselor: So, what did you think about your ultrasound, Erin?

Erin: Um, I don't know. OK, I guess.

Counselor: What did you see?

Erin: I saw a baby, my baby.

Counselor: How did that make you feel?

Erin: It doesn't matter. I can't keep it. My parents will hate me. My boyfriend will leave me. I need an abortion.

Counselor: I understand that pressure, I really do. Can I ask if you are a religious person?

Erin: Yeah, I go to church.

Counselor: OK. So you believe in God?

Erin: Yeah.

Counselor: Do you think He has something to say about abortion?

Erin: He wouldn't like it.

Counselor: Are you sure?

Erin: Pretty sure.

Counselor: So what would God say about your decision to abort?

Erin: He probably wouldn't like it. But I have to do it. I have no other options.

Counselor: How will God respond to that?

Erin: It doesn't matter. He'll forgive me. He forgives everyone, and He'll forgive me for this.

This conversation has been repeated over and over in life-affirming pregnancy centers across the United States. As we've already noted, a large majority of women who abort their children claim to be Protestant or Catholic, and a subset of those claim they go to church regularly. They believe in God. They believe He exists, that He creates life, and that He saves people from their sins. And they almost uniformly agree that God doesn't like abortion. But they abort their children anyway.

With so many Christians aborting their children, we must ask whether or not it is really wrong. Death, after all, is a prominent theme in the Bible. God killed people (His own Son came to die), and He authorized capital punishment in the Old Testament. In order to properly answer the question of whether God gives us the right to kill innocent life, we must understand when life actually begins, how God values life, the purpose of capital punishment, and God's commands regarding innocent life.

When Does Life Begin?

Let's qualify when life actually begins, both medically and biblically. Modern medicine has shown that human life begins at conception. There may be very subtle nuances when using the word "conception" in the cases of twinning or in vitro fertilization, and I acknowledge that fertilization may occur at slightly different times in those circumstances. For simplicity's sake, I'll use the term "conception" to cover fertilization even in those rare examples.

More than forty years ago, as noted earlier, the California Medical Society acknowledged the obvious in an editorial in its journal *California Medicine* when it referred to "the scientific fact, which everyone really knows, that human life begins at conception." Embryology textbooks recognize this fact in how they define the zygote:

> This cell, formed by the union of an ovum and a sperm (Gr. zyg tos, yoked together), represents the beginning of a human being. The common expression "fertilized ovum" refers to the zygote.[114]

For those interested in a more technical description:

> The chromosomes of the oocyte and sperm are . . . respectively enclosed within female and male pronuclei. These pronuclei fuse with each other to produce the

single, diploid, 2N nucleus of the fertilized zygote. This moment of zygote formation may be taken as the beginning or zero time point of embryonic development.[115]

That a unique human being springs to life at conception is no longer up for scientific debate:

Although life is a continuous process, fertilization is a critical landmark because, under ordinary circumstances, a new, genetically distinct human organism is thereby formed. . . . The combination of 23 chromosomes present in each pronucleus results in 46 chromosomes in the zygote. Thus the diploid number is restored and the embryonic genome is formed. The embryo now exists as a genetic unity.[116]

Yet another textbook describes the beginning of life this way: "Almost all higher animals start their lives from a single cell, the fertilized ovum (zygote). . . . The time of fertilization represents the starting point in the life history, or ontogeny, of the individual."[117]

For a very complete and detailed explanation of the beginning of life, I recommend the definitive work *Embryo: A Defense of Human Life*, by Robert P. George and Christopher Tollefsen.

Let's see if the Bible agrees with modern medicine about human life beginning at conception.

Conceived and Born

Scripture regularly speaks in terms of "conceived and bore" as the natural progression of life. Over thirty-five verses in the Old and New

Testament use a form of that phrase to indicate the beginning of life and its subsequent stages of maturity. The phrase "conceive and bore" appears fourteen times in Genesis alone.

The record of the very first child in utero, Cain, uses this convention: "Now the man had relations with his wife Eve, and she conceived and gave birth to Cain" (Genesis 4:1).

When the time finally came for the fulfillment of God's promise of a son to Abraham, "Sarah conceived and bore a son to Abraham in his old age, at the appointed time of which God had spoken to him" (Genesis 21:2).

Rachel, after years of barrenness, had her own prayers for children answered: "Then God remembered Rachel, and God gave heed to her and opened her womb. So she conceived and bore a son and said, 'God has taken away my reproach'" (Genesis 30:22–23). Her child was Joseph, the man who would save Egypt and his family from deadly famine.

Hosea clearly describes the natural progression of maturity in like fashion (though in reverse) pronouncing judgment on Ephraim (Israel):

> As for Ephraim, their glory will fly away like a bird—
> No birth, no pregnancy and no conception!
> Though they bring up their children,
> I will bereave them until not a man is left.
> Yes, woe to them indeed when I depart from them!
> (Hosea 9:11–12)

The theme of conception, pregnancy, and birth is carried throughout Scripture. There is no indication that an unborn child in the Old Testament was considered anything but a member of the human family and as valuable as those who were already born. In fact, barrenness was considered a curse, whereas pregnancy was considered a tremendous blessing.

Even in the Bible's original languages, it makes no distinction between the life of an unborn child and the life of one who's been born. *Yeled* is a Hebrew term in the Old Testament that refers to a child or a boy whether inside the womb or outside. The same principle that claims no distinction between born and unborn children as image-bearers of God is maintained in the New Testament as well. The Greek term *brephos* is used to refer to the young Hebrew males who were slaughtered at Pharaoh's command in Acts 7:17–19, as well as to an unborn John the Baptist who leapt at the presence of Jesus while they were both still in their mothers' wombs (Luke 1:41–44).

Of course, it's one thing to agree that life begins at conception scientifically and biblically. It's quite another to determine the value of life.

The abortion culture in America is fundamentally based on one simple premise: life inside the womb is worth less than life outside. Whether a child is aborted for financial reasons, relational pressure, inconvenience, disability, rape, or guilt, very few people would view the same factors as valid reasons for killing a toddler. And, as I noted earlier, the American church generally falls in line with the culture's thinking. Whether we admit it or not, the church's silence about abortion is approval of the devaluation of children in the womb.

Does God agree?

Incarnation

The cornerstone of the Christian faith is the life, death, and resurrection of Jesus Christ. Have you ever wondered why God didn't send Jesus to earth as a grown man? Why He didn't send Christ as a teenager or toddler? Why Jesus didn't arrive on a chariot of fire surrounded by angels?

Because Jesus was fully God and fully man. And, in order to claim his humanness, He came to earth in the same manner every other human being does—through conception:

> But when he had considered this, behold, an angel of the Lord appeared to him in a dream, saying, "Joseph, son of David, do not be afraid to take Mary as your wife; for the Child who has been conceived in her is of the Holy Spirit. She will bear a Son; and you shall call His name Jesus, for He will save His people from their sins." (Matt. 1:20–21)

We see the same theme here reflected everywhere else in the Bible. Jesus Christ, the very Son of God, was conceived and born.

If you contemplate the Incarnation in light of the sacredness of human life, it is revolutionary. The Savior of the world was conceived. We often say that Jesus came to earth as a baby. We tend to picture Jesus as a small baby, just born, lying in a manger. But even more startling is that He came as a zygote, grew into an embryo, then a fetus, then a full-sized baby.

I can think of no better reason to equate the value of life in the womb the same as life outside. God Himself came to earth, and He came as a zygote.

Life in the Womb

Job recognized that God created all human life in the womb and that He has an intimate knowledge of every human being. When comparing himself to slaves, Job explains:

If I have despised the claim of my male or female slaves

When they filed a complaint against me,

What then could I do when God arises?

And when He calls me to account, what will I answer Him?

Did not He who made me in the womb make him,

And the same one fashion us in the womb? (Job 31:13–15)

The Bible also shares stories of life and activity in the womb. Rebekah becomes pregnant with twins, and they were apparently very active unborn babies. She asks God why:

"If it is so, why then am I this way?" So she went to inquire of the LORD.

The LORD said to her, "Two nations are in your womb;

And two peoples will be separated from your body;

And one people shall be stronger than the other,

And the older shall serve the younger." (Gen. 25:22–23)

As with Christ, we see God has a distinct purpose for these little babies, and that plan begins to play out even before birth.

John the Baptist recognized his Savior from the safety and sanctity of the womb. When the pregnant Mary came to visit her pregnant cousin, Elizabeth, John the Baptist (in utero) jumped for joy:

When Elizabeth heard Mary's greeting, the baby leaped in her womb; and Elizabeth was filled with the Holy Spirit. And she cried out with a loud voice and said, "Blessed are you among women, and blessed is the fruit of your womb!" (Luke 1:41–42)

God Has Plans for Us

Clearly, life begins at conception according to Scripture, and life is cherished and treasured even in the womb. We also see a constant theme of God knowing and preordaining the role of biblical figures even before they come into existence.

Samson's mother had an angelic visit:

> Then the angel of the LORD appeared to the woman and said to her, "Behold now, you are barren and have borne no children, but you shall conceive and give birth to a son. Now therefore, be careful not to drink wine or strong drink, nor eat any unclean thing. For behold, you shall conceive and give birth to a son, and no razor shall come upon his head, for the boy shall be a Nazirite to God from the womb; and he shall begin to deliver Israel from the hands of the Philistines." (Judg. 13:3–5)

God spoke to Jeremiah about his role and made it clear that God's plans for him predated his birth:

> Before I formed you in the womb I knew you,
> And before you were born I consecrated you;
> I have appointed you a prophet to the nations. (Jer. 1:5)

Isaiah experienced God's foreknowledge and ordination of events in the womb, as He described when he wrote about the coming Savior:

> Listen to Me, O islands,
> And pay attention, you peoples from afar.

The LORD called Me from the womb;

From the body of My mother He named Me. (Isa. 49:1)

And now says the LORD, who formed Me from the womb to be His Servant,

To bring Jacob back to Him, so that Israel might be gathered to Him

(For I am honored in the sight of the LORD,

And My God is My strength). (Isa. 49:5)

Even Paul, the murderer of Christians-turned-apostle, recognized God's hand in his life at the earliest of stages:

But when God, who had set me apart even from my mother's womb and called me through His grace, was pleased to reveal His Son in me so that I might preach Him among the Gentiles. (Gal. 1:15–16)

Jesus Christ came to earth as a zygote. The Bible makes no textual distinction between life inside or outside the womb. Scripture shares insights into life in the womb, and it also reveals God has a purpose and plan for each new life.

Each and every unborn child is precious and purposeful.

A Problem Verse?

There is a passage in Exodus that is often quoted by pro-abortion advocates because some have incorrectly interpreted it to indicate that life in the womb is less valuable than life outside. While elaborating on the Ten Commandments, God provides the following instructions:

> If men struggle with each other and strike a woman with child so that she gives birth prematurely, yet there is no injury, he shall surely be fined as the woman's husband may demand of him, and he shall pay as the judges decide.
>
> But if there is any further injury, then you shall appoint as a penalty life for life, eye for eye, tooth for tooth, hand for hand, foot for foot, burn for burn, wound for wound, bruise for bruise. (Exod. 21:22–25)

Regarding this passage, theologian Wayne Grudem says, "For the question of abortion, perhaps the most significant passage of all is found in the specific laws God gave Moses for the people of Israel during the time of the Mosaic covenant."[118]

Questions arise when the phrase "gives birth prematurely" is rendered "miscarriage" as in the New Revised Standard version. The implication is that the child dies and the man has to just pay a fine, versus suffering capital punishment if the mother dies. The life of the child is therefore worth less because the punishment for that death is less than if the mother dies.

However, the Hebrew phrase is best translated as "to come out" and is translated "born prematurely" in the NASB, not "miscarriage." Also, verse 23 means that if there is any further injury to either party, the "eye for an eye" penalty arises. In other words, verse 22 means that a man is fined for a premature birth even if both mother and child are fine. If, however, either the woman or baby is hurt, the more severe penalty applies, up to and including the death penalty.

Hebrew scholar Gleason Archer states:

There is no ambiguity here whatever. What is required is that if there should be an injury either to the mother or to her children, the injury shall be avenged by a like injury to the assailant. If it involves the life . . . of the premature baby, then the assailant shall pay for it with his life. There is no second class status attached to the fetus under this rule; he is avenged just as if he were a normally delivered child or an older person: life for life.[119]

The fact that God's law imposed a "life for life" penalty on the unintentionally negligent homicide of an unborn child is highly significant. Wayne Grudem points out that "[i]n other cases in the Mosaic law where someone *accidentally* caused the death of another person, there was no requirement to give 'life for life,' no capital punishment." Such a person had the option to flee to a city of refuge where he or she would be safe.

Grudem concludes, "This means that God established for Israel a law code that placed a higher value on protecting the life of a pregnant woman and her preborn child than the life of anyone else in Israelite society. Far from treating the death of a preborn child as less significant than the death of others in society, this law treats the death of a preborn child or its mother as more significant and worthy of more severe punishment."[120]

Handicapped or Disabled Unborn Children

Over 90 percent of Down syndrome children are aborted in America today. Countless other children who test for some malady are killed before they ever have a chance to be born. But are children with a handicap, disability, or even a terminal condition less valuable than other children?

When Moses complained to God that he wasn't able to lead the people of Israel out of Egypt, God's response was:

> Who has made man's mouth? Or who makes him mute or deaf, or seeing or blind? Is it not I, the LORD? (Exod. 4:11)

When His disciples asked if a man born blind was being punished for his sins or his parents' sins, Jesus replied:

> It was neither that this man sinned, nor his parents; but it was so that the works of God might be displayed in him. (John 9:3)

Not only does the American church devalue life in the womb, we devalue life that doesn't meet our perfect expectations. However, the Bible is clear. Because of God's sovereignty over sin, death, genetic conditions, disease, and deformity, every human being possesses inherent dignity and value and is part of God's matchless plan.

What about Rape and Incest?

Many Christians believe unborn life should be protected unless the life is conceived through a horrible act such as rape or incest. Is a child conceived through a crime worth less than a child that isn't?

Rape and incest are unspeakable crimes against women. The emotional and physical damage can be severe, and they are both acts of exploitation by sinful people. Though the actual number of abortions attributed to rape and incest are minuscule compared to abortions for convenience, this remains a key point for the church to address.

The argument for abortion in the case of rape generally focuses on the emotional toll on the mother. Not only does she get pregnant through violence and without her consent, she is reminded of the crime each day through her pregnancy and potentially through the face of her child after birth. Through no fault of her own, she may face a constant reminder of her rape because of the pregnancy.

In the case of incest, the argument for abortion generally focuses on the potential genetic abnormalities or birth defects of the child. Plus consequences of incest on the family structure can be highly complex and emotionally damaging.

I don't know if there is a more emotionally charged piece of the abortion debate than rape cases. We all feel tremendous sympathy for the woman and typically feel hatred and disdain for the criminal. That we as Christians should extend compassion, help, justice, and care to the victims of these crimes is unquestioned.

Yet we must ask ourselves a difficult question: Was the crime a surprise to God?

God doesn't cause sin to happen. James makes that clear:

> Let no one say when he is tempted, "I am being tempted by God"; for God cannot be tempted by evil, and He Himself does not tempt anyone. (James 1:13)

We know, however, that God is the author of all life. Does He use heinous crimes to glorify Himself and bring about something beautiful? Is a new life conceived in sin a sin? Is he deserving of death because of the manner in which he was conceived? Or is God bringing about something beautiful even through the worst mankind has to offer? Does God ordain and bring about new life even if He loathes the sin that brought about conception?

These are very difficult and complex questions. Yet if we trust the Bible, we must conclude that God is the Author of all life, and He uses the worst in us to bring about newness and redemption. A baby is always a beautiful, redemptive reminder that new life can arise from the worst of circumstances.

Thus a life-affirming Christian believes that unborn children in the cases of rape and incest must be protected and have a right to live. This doesn't diminish the pain and suffering that those crimes cause, but it does mean the child should not receive the death penalty for a crime she didn't commit.

We must also be careful not to unwittingly convey a double standard with our biblical defense when it comes to rape and incest. Several denominations and many Christians believe abortion is wrong except in cases of rape and incest. In other words, a child has priceless value and the right to live in some circumstances but has less value and no right to live in others. This is the same moral and ethical mistake the pro-abortion movement makes. The "pro-choice" argument says that a child who is wanted and planned has tremendous value. A child who is unwanted and unplanned has less value. One has the right to live based on the desires of the parents; the other can be killed because of different desires of the parents.

When the Christian falls into the same temptation of assigning value based on circumstances rather than on Who authors life, we create a double standard. The child becomes a victim of a secular worldview instead of being recognized as a precious, beautiful creation of a creative God.

John Frame sums it up nicely: "There is nothing in Scripture that even remotely suggests that the unborn child is anything less than a human person from the moment of conception."[121]

Death as Punishment

We may be tempted to question the fact that life has tremendous value in light of the frequency of death in the Bible. God commanded the

Israelites in the Old Testament to wipe out entire cities and groups, including women and children, as they moved to inhabit Canaan, the Promised Land. Because of the Israelites' stubbornness and rejection of a Holy God, they were also punished with death during their journeys.

The story of David and Goliath, known worldwide as the ultimate underdog story, still resulted in the death of another human being (albeit a very large, evil one).

Elijah called the fire of heaven down upon a very wet altar as he dueled with 450 prophets of Baal. Baal didn't respond accordingly, and Elijah killed all 450 prophets.

The Holy Spirit took the lives of Ananias and Sapphira in the book of Acts for lying about their donation to the church. And God orchestrated the killing of His own Son in the most gruesome, horrific way invented by man—crucifixion. A more painful, bloody, malicious form of death was not found in ancient times, and yet this is the means by which God ordained His own Son to die. God allowed, instructed, and caused death throughout Scripture:

> The LORD kills and makes alive;
> He brings down to Sheol and raises up. (1 Sam. 2:6)

So is God a God of death or life?

In the Beginning . . .

While death is a theme in Scripture, do we serve a God who doles out death and is indiscriminate about life? On the contrary, the very first words of the Bible reveal a God who creates life:

> In the beginning God created the heavens and the earth.
> (Gen. 1:1)

The next thirty verses explode with a vivid, vibrant narrative of God moving over the earth, causing stars to burst forth in the sky, plants and animals to spring into existence on the earth, and newness to abound. It's as if a master artist is joyfully, almost playfully, painting a canvas with colors, shapes, and forms.

Life comes to the universe in extraordinary fashion. C. S. Lewis gives us an allegorical picture of creation in *The Magician's Nephew*. Aslan the Lion is giving birth to a new world:

> In all directions it [the earth] was swelling into humps. They were of very different sizes, some no bigger than molehills, some as big as wheelbarrows, two the size of cottages. All the humps moved and swelled till they burst, and the crumbled earth poured out of them, and from each hump there came out an animal. The moles came out just as you might see a mole come out in England. The dogs came out, barking the moment their heads were free, and struggling as you've seen them do when they are getting through a narrow hole in the hedge. The stags were the queerest to watch, for of course the antlers came up a long time before the rest of them. . . . The frogs, who all came up near the river, went straight into it with a plop-plop and a loud croaking. The panthers, leopards and things of that sort, sat down at once to wash the loose earth off their hind quarters and then stood up against the trees to

sharpen their front claws. Showers of birds came out of the trees. Butterflies fluttered. Bees got to work on the flowers as if they hadn't a second to lose. But the greatest moment of all was when the biggest hump broke like a small earthquake and out came the sloping back, the large, wise head, and the four baggy-trousered legs of an elephant.[122]

On the sixth day in Genesis, God forms the crown of creation: man.

> Then God said, "Let Us make man in Our image, according to Our likeness; and let them rule over the fish of the sea and over the birds of the sky and over the cattle and over all the earth, and over every creeping thing that creeps on the earth." God created man in His own image, in the image of God He created him; male and female He created them. God blessed them; and God said to them, "Be fruitful and multiply, and fill the earth, and subdue it; and rule over the fish of the sea and over the birds of the sky and over every living thing that moves on the earth." Then God said, "Behold, I have given you every plant yielding seed that is on the surface of all the earth, and every tree which has fruit yielding seed; it shall be food for you; and to every beast of the earth and to every bird of the sky and to every thing that moves on the earth which has life, I have given every green plant for food"; and it was so. God saw all that He had made, and behold, it was very

good. And there was evening and there was morning, the sixth day. (Gen. 1:26–31)

This passage is chock-full of wonder and insight. God created us in His image, He designed us to rule over the rest of creation, He blessed us and called us to be fruitful, and He provided sustenance for our livelihood.

It's also important to note that God didn't just create man and leave us in a vacuum. He created human life, but He also provided us with purpose, provision, and relationship to give us abundant life.

Purpose:
We were created to rule over creation and have dominion.

Provision:
He provided food for us to eat so we could continue living.

Relationship:
Unique in all creation is the relationship between God and man. We were made to have a relationship with the Creator. God then gave Eve to Adam, forming the first marriage and promise of a family.

All of our needs—physical, spiritual, and relational—were met through the original act of creation. God is the Author of Life and provided for eternal, abundant, perfect life on that sixth day. That's the beginning of the story—a God who creates us out of nothing and places us in a perfect environment where we can enjoy life in all of its abundance with Him and for Him.

In the End . . .

Although this breaks my rule of not skipping to the end of a book, let's jump to the end of the Bible to see how the Creator God wraps up human history. In Revelation 22, God paints a picture of the end of history that is marvelous and ineffable. After John describes a majestic city descending from the heavens, he gives us just a glimpse of eternity:

> Then he showed me a river of the water of life, clear as crystal, coming from the throne of God and of the Lamb, in the middle of its street. On either side of the river was the tree of life, bearing twelve kinds of fruit, yielding its fruit every month; and the leaves of the tree were for the healing of the nations. There will no longer be any curse; and the throne of God and of the Lamb will be in it, and His bond-servants will serve Him; they will see His face, and His name will be on their foreheads. And there will no longer be any night; and they will not have need of the light of a lamp nor the light of the sun, because the Lord God will illumine them; and they will reign forever and ever. (Rev. 22:1–5)

We see perfection yet again, but this time the perfection is permanent and even more spectacular: a crystal river; trees bearing eternal, healing fruit; no threat of sin or death; no darkness; eternal joy in perfect relationship with one another and with God.

We are eternal beings:

> He has made everything appropriate in its time. He has also set eternity in their heart, yet so that man will

not find out the work which God has done from the beginning even to the end. (Eccles. 3:11)

And one day we will realize eternity in all of its glory, as life more abundant than we can ever imagine.

The Bible opens and closes with a God who creates, provides for, and sustains human life. He created us to have fellowship with Him, and He tells us that one day we will enjoy Him forever. The beginning and end embody life, joy, and perfection. It's the middle part that gets messy.

Life and Death

God did not create death when He spent six days bringing something out of nothing. His instructions to Adam show that God created an ideal environment for him, free from death:

> Then the LORD God took the man and put him into the garden of Eden to cultivate it and keep it. The LORD God commanded the man, saying, "From any tree of the garden you may eat freely; but from the tree of the knowledge of good and evil you shall not eat, for in the day that you eat from it you will surely die." (Gen. 2:15–17)

It only took a short time, however, for Adam and Eve to break God's commandment, and through their sin, death entered the world. God provided a choice for Adam and Eve: life or death. Death was God's judgment for sin, and they chose death.

And here is a crucial point: God is sovereign over all things, and that includes death. Death entered the world because of Adam's sin and is still subject to God's control. God cursed man, because of sin, to die, according to the commandment He gave.

After death is introduced through sin, it doesn't take long for man to take the power of life and death into his own hands. Adam and Eve's son, Cain, kills his brother, Abel, in Genesis 4. God's response to Cain displays God's love for life:

> He said, "What have you done? The voice of your brother's blood is crying to Me from the ground." (Gen. 4:10)

God punishes Cain immediately, showing that His desire is for life to be protected. He condemns Cain to a life of wandering the earth. After Cain complains that his punishment may lead to his own death, God shows yet again His plan to protect life, even the life of a murderer:

> So the LORD said to him, "Therefore whoever kills Cain, vengeance will be taken on him sevenfold." And the LORD appointed a sign for Cain, so that no one finding him would slay him. (Gen. 4:15)

Thus we see both the judgment and mercy of God. He disciplines and protects Cain at the same time.

Because of sin and evil, God used death as a form of judgment. The most notable example of this judgment is the Flood. God's wrath is kindled because of the global evil and lawlessness of man:

> Now the earth was corrupt in the sight of God, and the earth was filled with violence. God looked on the

earth, and behold, it was corrupt; for all flesh had corrupted their way upon the earth. Then God said to Noah, "The end of all flesh has come before Me; for the earth is filled with violence because of them; and behold, I am about to destroy them with the earth." (Gen. 6:11–13)

Even through this judgment, God again preserves and protects life. This time He protects just a small group of the human race and members of the animal kingdom.

After the Flood, God reemphasizes the preeminence of life in His covenant with Noah:

Whoever sheds man's blood,
By man his blood shall be shed,
For in the image of God
He made man. (Gen. 9:6)

God so values human life that He institutes capital punishment. The ultimate deterrent for murder is the threat of losing what is most precious to us—our lives.

This is a key point: there are times in biblical history when evil, corruption, violence, and abuse are so pervasive, God exercises punishment by death in order to protect and preserve life. It's also important to remember that while God at times used death as a form of judgment in an immediate sense, we will all die because of sin. The consequence of sin is death. We all sin, thus we all physically die. So while God accelerated death at times as a form of immediate judgment, "natural" death has come to all because of sin.

Christ has removed the sting and fear of death for Christians, and death for us is a passing into a blessed eternal life. Because of Christ, we escape the punishment of death, though we will all experience it.

God, Children, and Innocent Blood

God established a summary of moral law in Exodus through the Ten Commandments. Though the last five commandments are written as negatives ("Thou shalt not"), they assume the related positive rights.

- "You shall not murder" protects the right to life.
- "You shall not commit adultery" protects the fidelity of the core community relationship—marriage.
- "You shall not steal" protects personal property.
- "You shall not bear false witness against your neighbor" protects the integrity and name of others.
- "You shall not covet" protects our hearts from selfishness and envy.

Notice the order of the last five commands: protect life, protect marriage, protect property, protect our name, and protect our hearts. If we don't have the right to live, the rest of the commandments are irrelevant. Mankind is to do all it can to protect and preserve life. In biblical times, this included capital punishment for severe crimes in order to maintain that protection for others.

But what about those who have not committed a crime and have not caused violence? Does God have direction for us regarding innocent people and children?

In Proverbs 6, the writer gives us insight into the heart of God:

> There are six things which the LORD hates.
>
> Yes, seven which are an abomination to Him:
>
> Haughty eyes, a lying tongue,
>
> And hands that shed innocent blood,
>
> A heart that devises wicked plans,
>
> Feet that run rapidly to evil,
>
> A false witness who utters lies,
>
> And one who spreads strife among brothers.
>
> (Prov. 6:16–19)

God hates "hands that shed innocent blood," a theme we see throughout the Bible.

Among the cultures in the Old Testament period, child sacrifice, mutilation, great atrocities against other nations, and sexual perversion were common. One of the primary reasons God commanded Israel to destroy other nations as they began to take over the Promised Land was violence against children. As Moses is giving his last sermons and instructions as described in Deuteronomy, he reminds the people of Israel:

> When the LORD your God cuts off before you the nations which you are going in to dispossess, and you dispossess them and dwell in their land, beware that you are not ensnared to follow them, after they are destroyed before you, and that you do not inquire after their gods, saying, "How do these nations serve their gods, that I also may do likewise?"
>
> You shall not behave thus toward the LORD your God, for every abominable act which the LORD hates

they have done for their gods; for they even burn
their sons and daughters in the fire to their gods.
(Deut. 12:29–31)

Notice the use of the word "even" to illustrate the extremity of this
evil. Child sacrifice is evil in its worst form.

And at times, God's chosen people, the Israelites, were influenced
by those nations. In Psalm 106, the psalmist recounts the history of
the nation of Israel, showing that the Israelites regularly forgot God's
goodness and His direction. They allowed themselves to engage in vile
practices because they intermingled with destructive nations. Though
God went to great lengths to protect life, the Israelites began to take
innocent life themselves, ignoring God's commands:

They also provoked Him to wrath at the waters of
Meribah,
So that it went hard with Moses on their account;
Because they were rebellious against His Spirit,
He spoke rashly with his lips.
They did not destroy the peoples,
As the LORD commanded them,
But they mingled with the nations
And learned their practices,
And served their idols,
Which became a snare to them.
They even sacrificed their sons and their daughters to
the demons,
And shed innocent blood,
The blood of their sons and their daughters,

Whom they sacrificed to the idols of Canaan;

And the land was polluted with the blood.

(Ps. 106:32–38)

Note that the theme of innocent blood is often linked to children. Children are the primary victims of injustice, violence, and crime. They are the weakest among us, and they have virtually no ability to defend themselves from verbal, physical, or emotional attacks.

God has a special affinity for children:

> But when Jesus saw this, He was indignant and said to them, "Permit the children to come to Me; do not hinder them; for the kingdom of God belongs to such as these. Truly I say to you, whoever does not receive the kingdom of God like a child will not enter it at all." And He took them in His arms and began blessing them, laying His hands on them. (Mark 10:14–16)

Throughout the entirety of Scripture, children are a sign of tremendous blessing and favor. God commanded Adam and Eve to "be fruitful and multiply" in the Cultural Mandate (Genesis 1:28). After the flood, God reiterated this blessing to Noah:

> As for you, be fruitful and multiply;
> Populate the earth abundantly and multiply in it.
> (Gen. 9:7)

Abraham was promised he would be the father of many nations:

And He took him outside and said, "Now look toward
the heavens, and count the stars, if you are able to count
them." And He said to him, "So shall your descendants
be." (Gen. 15:5)

The psalmist emphasizes the blessing of children:

Behold, children are a gift of the LORD,
The fruit of the womb is a reward.
Like arrows in the hand of a warrior,
So are the children of one's youth.
How blessed is the man whose quiver is full of them;
They will not be ashamed
When they speak with their enemies in the gate.
(Ps. 127:3–5)

Let's return to our original question: If God is sovereign and the
author of all life, does He give man the right to kill innocent life? What
can we conclude?

1. God is a God of life. The Bible begins and ends with a beautiful
   picture of a world where life is created, sustained, and lived
   abundantly through God's grace and provision.
2. God is sovereign over death. Death came into the world through
   sin. And somehow, God still uses it for His glory.
3. Because of the depth of evil and sin in the world, God has used
   death as a means of punishment for grievous sins, often as a
   means of protecting and preserving life.
4. At the same time, He has been abundantly clear that man is to
   protect innocent life, not take it. Throughout Scripture, God

commands us to keep ourselves from shedding innocent blood and to protect those weakest among us.

5. God has a special affinity for children, born or unborn. They are a blessing and a sign of God's favor.

God does not give us the right to abort our children. In fact, to abort a child is to grieve the heart of God. Unborn children are guilty of no crime. They have not caused violence and they have not harmed others. They are weak, frail, and completely dependent on others for their welfare. We are to protect innocent human life, not kill it.

Solomon summed up this foundational truth in Ecclesiastes 8:8:

No man has authority to restrain the wind with the wind, or authority over the day of death; and there is no discharge in the time of war, and evil will not deliver those who practice it.

CHAPTER 6

Should the Church Protect Innocent Life?

I sat back in my chair, trying to process what I had just read.

"The mother chose life and, more importantly, she accepted Christ!"

The note was in an email from a pro-life pregnancy center in a southern state. Our organization, Online for Life, works cooperatively with this and numerous other pro-life clinics across the country, collaborating to rescue babies and families from abortion.

The sentence was innocent enough, and I'm sure it was written with joy and gratitude for what God had done that day in the counseling room. But as I sat there rereading the comment, I thought to myself, *Was it really more important that the mom accepted Christ, or that a baby was rescued from being ripped limb from limb in the womb? Should we be more excited about a prayer of salvation or a tiny life rescued from an unjust death?*

It's not hard to defend her line of reasoning. To lead someone to Christ is to witness a person rescued from eternal death and ushered into a life of joy. We know, as followers of Christ, the unspeakable blessings of being a part of the Body of Christ, both in this life and the next.

Yet something still gnawed at me. If the mother accepted Christ but still aborted her baby, would we still have a sense of gratitude and satisfaction? Do we as Christians accept that outcome (which is unfortunately common) as a win/win because the mother is saved from hell and we presume the child is ushered into heaven?

In light of the last two chapters, I confess I struggle with this dilemma. It seems to me that much of evangelical Protestantism has come to believe that the only responsibility of the church is to save souls, yet many Catholic churches excel at mercy ministry and liberal mainline churches tend toward social justice.

What is the proper balance? And what is the role of the church?

Converts vs. Disciples

I wonder how many American Christians believe our primary purpose on this planet is to tell people that Jesus died for them. While it is obviously true that Jesus died for our sins, is that all He did? Is the entire message of the gospel that, because of Christ's life, death, and resurrection, we can go to heaven if we accept Him?

Christ summed up His instructions for His church in the Great Commission:

> And Jesus came up and spoke to them, saying, "All authority has been given to Me in heaven and on earth. Go therefore and make disciples of all the nations, baptizing them in the name of the Father and the Son and the Holy Spirit, teaching them to observe all that I commanded you; and lo, I am with you always, even to the end of the age." (Matt. 28:18–20)

Let's extract a few key principles from Jesus's command.

1. Christ reasserts His omnipotence and sovereignty: "All authority . . . in heaven and earth." Jesus is in complete control over everything in the universe. This aligns with our previous study of God's sovereignty.

2. Christ commands His followers to "go and make disciples of all nations."

3. Christ instructs His followers to "teach them to observe all that I have commanded you," which presumably includes everything Jesus taught in the New Testament as well as what He affirmed that was previously recorded (the Old Testament).

4. Christ reaffirms His continuing presence and sustaining power by the Father's eventually sending the Holy Spirit: "I am with you always, even to the end of the age."

In American Christianity, we often assume that our church's primary purpose is evangelism, which usually means sharing the message of salvation and praying for converts. But notice the Great Commission does not instruct us to make converts—Christ instructs us to make *disciples.* What is the difference between a convert and a disciple?

According to Merriam-Webster, to convert someone means to "bring over from one's belief, view, or party to another" or "to bring about a religious conversion in." A disciple is "one who accepts and assists in spreading the doctrines of another."

There is an important distinction here. A convert has to do with an event, a moment in time, or a process. It is moving a person from one set of beliefs to another. There is a beginning and an end to conversion, and there is a sense of a temporary relationship to the word. If we make one convert, it's time to move on to the next.

The term "disciple" (a follower, pupil, learner) has an ongoing, long-term, relational sense to it. If we are growing as disciples, we are engaging in constant, rigorous training over a long period of time. We submit to the discipline and teaching of another.

If you've ever attempted to lose weight like I have, you understand the difference between conversion and discipline. Let's say you are introduced to a new diet plan that promises weight loss, renewed energy, and vitality. This program includes a nutritional plan, supplements, and an exercise regimen. You like what you see, so you decide to adopt the program. You are, in effect, converted. You make a decision to reject your current attitudes, habits, and beliefs about your weight and embrace a new set.

Now comes the discipline. In order for the diet program to work, you need to embrace these changes over a long period of time, usually measured in months. And if you want to keep the weight off, the disciplines you've adopted need to be permanent. One must be converted in order to become a disciple, but they are two very different concepts.

American evangelical Christianity, at least for the past half-century or so, has been obsessed with making converts. Sermons, TV and radio messages, Internet ministry, tracts, evangelism training, and a host of other programs have focused almost exclusively on sharing the Good News about Jesus dying for us so that we might have eternal life. This is very good news indeed. But if the message ends there, on that we find salvation in Jesus Christ, we are not making disciples. We are making converts.

Making disciples means rigorous training. It means teaching, debating, discussing. It means challenging, rebuking, encouraging. It means digging deep into the Bible with another over an extended period of time.

What does discipleship look like? The four gospels and the book of Acts give us a deep and wide picture. Jesus modeled discipleship for the three years of His earthly ministry and discipleship expanded after Pentecost. Intense prayer, constant teaching, practical application, correction, training, and modeling loving, caring service—these are some of the aspects of discipleship that Christ displayed with His own small, ragtag group of followers.

What are the consequences of focusing on converts and not on making disciples? We begin to believe that the gospel is all about us. We begin to believe that the personal plan of salvation is the entirety of our faith. We begin to believe our only mission is to escape hell through Christ.

Let's turn to our third observation of the Great Commission. Jesus instructs His followers to teach the nations to observe all He has commanded them. What does "all" entail? It certainly includes everything in red letters in your Bible, and it also includes the entirety of Scripture as it applies today. Did Jesus teach us how to evangelize? He certainly did. Did He command us to share the Good News? Yes.

What else did He command and teach us to do? Did He teach us about marriage, sexuality, money, living in community, conflict resolution, how to relate to government, parenting, work, rest, play, prayer, and service? Indeed He did. And the grand summary of Christ's commands are summed up in Matthew 22:37–40:

> "YOU SHALL LOVE THE LORD YOUR GOD WITH ALL YOUR HEART, AND WITH ALL YOUR SOUL, AND WITH ALL YOUR MIND." This is the great and foremost commandment. The second is like it, "YOU SHALL LOVE YOUR NEIGHBOR AS YOURSELF." On these two commandments depend the whole Law and the Prophets.

The command of Christ is to love God and each other. Jesus taught us how to live in a relationship with God. He also taught much on how to live with each other.

To make disciples is to consistently, lovingly, and committedly teach and show others how to love God and each other. That is the primary call of the American church. And it extends to all aspects of life, inside and outside the local church. That's because Christians are part of a kingdom, and our King reigns over every speck of the universe.

The Gospel of the Kingdom

When Christians use the term "gospel" (meaning "good news"), I find they often mean the personal plan of salvation. Christ died, rose, and ascended, and if we accept Him as Lord and Savior, we have eternal life in Him.

As we've just explored, however, disciple-making is more than conversion, thus the gospel is more than the personal plan of salvation. Consider the exhilarating text in Colossians 1:

> For He rescued us from the domain of darkness, and transferred us to the kingdom of His beloved Son, in whom we have redemption, the forgiveness of sins. He is the image of the invisible God, the firstborn of all creation. For by Him all things were created, both in the heavens and on earth, visible and invisible, whether thrones or dominions or rulers or authorities—all things have been created through Him and for Him. He is before all things, and in Him all things hold together. He is also head of the body, the church; and He is the beginning, the firstborn from the dead, so that He

Himself will come to have first place in everything. For it was the Father's good pleasure for all the fullness to dwell in Him, and through Him to reconcile all things to Himself, having made peace through the blood of His cross; through Him, I say, whether things on earth or things in heaven. (Col. 1:13–20)

Entire books could be (and have been) written on Paul's exposition of the supremacy of Christ in Colossians. Let's consider just a few nuggets.

In verse 13 we see a fascinating description of salvation. By His blood, we are rescued and transferred. We are rescued from the domain of darkness and moved to the kingdom of Christ. Here we see salvation as more than a personal matter. Both the words "domain" and "kingdom" refer to regions that are ruled by someone. There is a sense that we are rescued out of one group into another. We are not rescued in isolation. Certainly we are rescued individually, but we are rescued and placed into a kingdom with others (indeed, with multitudes).

Paul goes on to describe the complete and magnificent supremacy of Jesus. He is the Imago Dei (image of God) and the first of all creation. (All humans are made *in* the image of God. Jesus *is* the Image of God). All things were created through Him, and He rules over all. He is in and through all, and holds all things together. He is truly the King of kings.

After showing Christ's supremacy over the created order, Paul reminds us that Christ is also the head of the church, the first to be resurrected, and He is first among all. He is King of the physical realm as well as the spiritual.

Verse 20 gives us insight into what the kingdom mentioned in verse 13 is all about. Christ has come to reconcile all things to Himself. If repetition is the key to learning, Paul ensures we are clear about what Christ has supremacy over. "All" or "all things" appears seven times in eight verses.

In their book, *When Helping Hurts*, Steve Corbett and Brian Fikkert remark,

> In this passage Jesus Christ is described as the Creator, Sustainer, and Reconciler of *everything*. Yes, Jesus died for our souls, but He also died to reconcile—that is, to put into right relationship—all that He created. . . . The curse is cosmic in scope, bringing decay, brokenness, and death to every speck of the universe. But as King of kings and Lord of lords, Jesus is making all things new! This is the good news of the gospel.
>
> The curse of sin breaks four relationships: our relationship with God, with ourselves, with others, and with creation. Christ came to reconcile all four relationships. It starts with our relationship with God, but He also redeems the other three. Christ not only preached salvation (our relationship with God), he healed people physically and emotionally (relationship with self), taught us how to live in marriage and community (relationship with others), and how to manage ourselves and the rest of the created order (relationship with creation).[123]

Consider how abortion relates to the curse Corbett and Fikkert describe:

- Our relationship with God: abortion is a sign of our rejection of our relationship with God. We spurn the beauty of His creation, just as Cain did in Genesis.

- Our relationship with self: three of the most sorrowful side effects of abortion are guilt, shame, and depression. Abortion has been linked to numerous physical and emotional conditions, including suicide, drug and alcohol abuse, mental and emotional disorders, and problems with self-image.

- Our relationship with others: abortion has also been clearly identified as a destroyer of relationships. Marriages are ruined, families are torn apart, boyfriends and girlfriends break up. Hurting people hurt people, and a post-abortive parent often damages other relationships.

- Our relationship with creation: abortion takes the life of another person. Instead of stewarding God's created human being, that human being is destroyed.

Yet in this kingdom Paul talks about, Christ reigns over all and is perpetually about the business of reconciling, restoring, and redeeming all things. What does this mean for a Christian today? What does it mean to be a child of the kingdom of God? Is the sense of a kingdom just an idea that shows up once in Colossians?

In fact, the theme of the kingdom of Christ is pervasive throughout the New Testament. Matthew's favorite variation is the "kingdom of heaven." He uses it thirty-two times in his gospel. For example:

- John the Baptist announced the arrival of Jesus with the exclamation, "Repent, for the kingdom of heaven is at hand" (Matt. 3:2).

- After Christ's temptation, He set out to begin His three-year ministry. What were His first words? "From that time Jesus began to preach and say, 'Repent, for the kingdom of heaven is at hand'" (Matt. 4:17).

- When Jesus began sending out His disciples in Matthew chapter 10, He said, "And as you go, preach, saying, 'The kingdom of heaven is at hand.' Heal the sick, raise the dead, cleanse the lepers, cast out demons. Freely you received, freely give" (Matt. 10:7–8).

Note the content of His instructions: preach the plan of salvation of Christ *and* reconcile and redeem physical and emotional illness. Christ came to reconcile all things.

Jesus began various parables in Matthew with "the kingdom of heaven is like. . . ." Mark and Luke also speak of the kingdom, and they used the term "kingdom of God."

Christian apologist Michael Craven remarks,

Today when evangelicals speak of the gospel, they almost always mean, simply, the personal plan of salvation. This is generally limited to an activity in which we present people with some facts about Jesus, ask them to agree with these facts, and if they do, instruct them to invite him into their lives or pray the sinner's prayer. Once they do this, we tell them, "You are saved!" And this, we teach, is the Christian's highest calling and fullest expression of the Christian faith.

We've heard this version of the gospel so many times that we don't even bother to question it—we simply accept it as "the gospel." However, when we put aside our culturally induced conceptions and study the scriptures, we discover that we have unwittingly embraced a truncated version of the gospel whose real-life implications are almost entirely private and centered on ourselves. In truth, the gospel, according to Scripture, focuses far less on Jesus' substitutionary death for us and being born again—and much more on his kingdom. In fact, Jesus only mentions the term born again one time in the Gospels and that was during his meeting with Nicodemus. However, Jesus mentions the kingdom 108 times! Even here, Jesus' mention of being born again points Nicodemus to the kingdom. Jesus says, "Truly, truly, I say to you, unless one is born again [also translated, from above] he cannot see the kingdom of God" (John 3:3). Jesus is explaining that unless one is born from above—an act of God that precedes any action of man he cannot partake of the kingdom. In other words, he cannot possess, he cannot see, and he cannot enjoy the rule and reign of God both now and throughout eternity.[124]

What we need to avoid is a "reductionist Gospel." We've reduced the gospel to nothing more than fire insurance. We accept Christ to escape hell and then go live our lives on our own terms, calling on Christ when we need him. This is the tragic downside of a church that is focused on conversion evangelism. We make converts, but we do not make disciples of the kingdom.

One might be tempted to claim that the kingdom of God is not a present reality. Christ came to save souls in this age and won't reconcile everything else until eternity. The church should be about saving souls now, and Christ will bring everything else to peace at the end of time. This view doesn't align with Scripture, especially since John the Baptist and Jesus both claimed that the kingdom of heaven was "at hand."

There is a sense in Scripture that the kingdom is "already but not yet." Christ brought the kingdom to bear on earth when He came to earth as a man. His kingdom has continued to increase and multiply ever since, and His reconciliation and redemption continue to grow. Yet we know that all is not well with the world—far from it. So the fulfillment of His kingdom is still in the future.

But today, right now, all those who follow Christ are children of His kingdom, and we are to be about His kingdom's work. And though the plan of salvation is central to that work, there is much, much more to be done.

The Church and Society

Numerous books have been written chronicling the church's involvement in all aspects of society since the first century. Throughout time, Christians have been heavily involved in reconciling and redeeming every part of society, whether it be law, arts, education, government, medicine, or science.

Today in America, we have a wide chasm separating church and state. I wrote about this in some detail in a previous book titled *Media Revolution: A Battle Plan to Defeat Mass Deception in America.* Our founding fathers never intended for the church to be removed from society (including government), nor does the term "separation of church and state" appear in any founding documents. It was a phrase taken from a letter from Thomas Jefferson to some Baptist friends, assuring them that government would not infringe on their worship. In other words, England's establishment of a national state religion would not occur in America. The state would stay out of the church's way.

A few hundred years of so-called "Enlightenment" thinking have reversed the original meaning of the phrase, and many people (including Christians) think it is a good idea for the church to stay out of all matters not related directly to evangelism or caring for the poor.

One of the champions of evangelism in the last half of the twentieth century was Dr. D. James Kennedy. He founded Evangelism Explosion, a lay evangelism training program that has been adopted worldwide. Dr. Kennedy was passionate for evangelism—and discipleship—but he had another passion for which he became much more well-known: Christian cultural involvement. Dr. Kennedy, who passed away in 2007, was a regularly-quoted voice calling for a return to righteousness in our nation and for greater engagement on the part of believers on concerns like the sanctity of human life and the sanctity of marriage.

In fact, a nationally known columnist once charged that Dr. Kennedy had "strayed from traditional preaching and focused primarily on politics and social issues."[125] I served at the time as the chief executive of Dr. Kennedy's broadcast ministry and responded that Dr. Kennedy believed "that we have a biblical responsibility to bring all of God's truth to bear on all of life."[126]

Dr. Kennedy, the senior pastor at Fort Lauderdale's Coral Ridge Presbyterian Church for almost fifty years, believed that Christians have twin obligations to obey the Great Commission and the "Cultural Mandate." That's the original command God gave to Adam and Eve in the Garden when he told them to "[b]e fruitful and multiply, and fill the earth, and subdue it; and rule over the fish of the sea and over the birds of the sky and over every living thing that moves on the earth" (Gen. 1:28).

The Cultural Mandate, Dr. Kennedy said, means "that we are to impact our culture for Christ in every facet of it while we are here in this world." It is "simply the redemption, not only of men, but all of the works of man, which are called culture, and all of the things man has created and has, so that this impacts every facet of man's life in this world. That is the Cultural Mandate we are to perform as well as the Great Commission."[127]

And while some in the modern church have a narrow notion of Christianity that limits the church's function to only evangelism, Dr. Kennedy pointed out in one of his most well-known books *What If Jesus Had Never Been Born?* that Christians have been impacting culture for good for almost two thousand years. Along with co-author Jerry Newcombe, Dr. Kennedy chronicled the positive influence of Christ's followers in just about every arena of human enterprise: education, civil liberty, economics, the family, medicine, the arts, and the value of human life.

Here is just one example regarding abortion and infanticide. Both were common in the ancient world, as noted earlier, but Christians aggressively opposed these practices, so much so that Roman emperor Valentinian outlawed infanticide in 374 A.D. He did so after heavy lobbying from Bishop Basil of Caesarea. As Kennedy and Newcombe wrote, "From transforming the value of human life to transforming individual lives, the positive impact of Jesus Christ is felt around the globe."[128]

The Church as Protector

Our brief journey through Scripture has led us to conclude that God is the creator of each and every human being. There is no such thing as an unplanned pregnancy in the will of God, and He doesn't make mistakes. A conceived child, regardless of race, gender, economic situation, handicap, or family situation is a gift from God, and God has a unique plan for each child. Man does not have the right to kill innocent life. God forbids it because He created us in His very own image.

Much of American evangelical Christianity in the last hundred years has incorrectly boiled down the gospel to one task: telling people that Jesus died for them and that they can go to heaven. While true, this "reductionist" gospel has led to a pronounced withdrawal of the church from the culture, which in turn has led to the secularization of virtually all aspects of society. Today the church no longer feels it has a voice in the overall culture because it voluntarily left in the first place.

Yet as the gospel of the kingdom instructs us, we are to be disciple-makers, teaching all that Christ commanded. That encompasses the entire Bible, which contains principles for all aspects of life, society, and culture. The kingdom of God is a present and future reality, and as His church, we are to be agents of His kingdom in all facets of society.

So let's get to specifics regarding abortion and innocent life. Does the Bible specifically command Christians to be actively and passionately involved in the protection of innocent life? And if so, does it just address a few Christians, or is protecting life an obligation of the entire church?

My father recently attended a local seminary course at his church about Christians and ethics. A young seminary student was addressing the group, and he brought up the subject of abortion.

"While I don't think the institution of the church should address the topic of abortion, I do support each layperson who works to protect life."

Not one to leave such a comment unattended, my father raised his hand and politely asked, "So are you saying that a pastor or church leader should never preach or teach about abortion?"

The student replied, "Yes, it should be something that individuals engage in if they feel so led."

Dad followed up, "So is it your position that the life of the mother is more valuable, biblically speaking, than the life of the unborn child?"

The young man was caught a bit off guard. "Uh, no, I'm not saying that."

And the subject was quickly changed.

This is a very popular view in many churches and denominations. As Rev. Dean Nelson, a founding member of the National Black Pro-life Coalition, told me, "Most seminaries tell seminarians to avoid talking or teaching about abortion. They consider it too volatile and political to address in their church. There is virtually no coursework, material, or texts on abortion in most seminaries."

I have a friend who works in a large church. Last year she was telling me how their church was implementing an exciting, comprehensive approach to discipleship. Hallmarks of the initiative include hundreds of pages of relevant content, a personal one-on-one approach, and a long-term commitment of the church to linking arms with people in the community. I thought it sounded like a fantastic way to spread the gospel.

"So this initiative involves a multi-month relationship with the person being discipled?" I asked her.

"Yes," she replied. "A mentor works with a person for several months, going through custom manuals and materials that are centered on giving a person a strong, foundational understanding of the Bible and the Christian life."

"That is awesome," I said. "Does the material cover anything on marriage?"

"Yup."

"How about pornography?"

"Yes, there is material about what we choose to view and take into our minds."

"Money management?"

"Yes," she said.

"Parenting?"

"Yeah, we discuss parenting."

"How about abortion?" I asked.

A long pause followed. "No."

"There isn't one word about abortion in a multi-volume, comprehensive program designed to train individuals about the Bible, the Christian life, and discipleship?"

"No."

"Abortion is an American holocaust. We lose a child every twenty-five seconds to abortion in our nation. It has more impact on the American Christian family than any other factor in history. Why doesn't the material cover it?" I inquired.

"I don't know," she replied.

My friend is a strong believer in the sacredness of human life. My friend's church is a life-affirming congregation. The senior pastor and church leadership are very vocal about protecting the unborn, and they strongly support life-affirming initiatives in their area. They do far more for unborn children and families than most churches.

Why then does their hallmark discipleship curriculum not include one word about the church and abortion?

Though the Bible clearly shows God's sovereignty at work in the creation of human life, maybe the Bible doesn't directly command us to protect human life. Maybe that's God's job.

As with every other area of life, God's Word is not silent. Scripture uses both positive and negative commands to provide us with direction.

We see from Genesis 4 that God cursed Cain for taking his brother's innocent life.

The same idea is expressed very clearly in chapter nine when God speaks to Noah.

God introduces the "eye for an eye" principle, indicating that the price for taking a life is another life. He immediately follows the principle with the restated command to be fruitful and multiply. God is a God of life, and He desires for life to grow and develop.

God's punishment for taking an innocent life is so severe (the criminal losing his own life), He shows that His design is for life to be protected at all costs. The most direct command to protect innocent life is, of course, in the Ten Commandments. Commandment six simply says, "You shall not murder." One might be tempted to determine that, as long as we as Christians do not take innocent lives, we are fulfilling our obligations.

Not so. Scripture calls us not only to avoid killing, it calls us directly to protect those in harm's way:

> If you are slack in the day of distress,
> Your strength is limited.
> Deliver those who are being taken away to death,
> And those who are staggering to slaughter,
> Oh hold them back.
> If you say, "See, we did not know this,"
> Does He not consider it who weighs the hearts?
> And does He not know it who keeps your soul?
> And will He not render to man according to his work?
> (Prov. 24:10–12)

Solomon's commands are in the positive tone. Instead of saying "don't," he tells us "do."

Does this command apply to unborn children and their families? Are unborn children being delivered to death? Are their families staggering to slaughter?

This passage in Proverbs is our core verse at Online for Life. God calls us to "deliver" and "save." Christians are to be actively engaged in rescuing other people from injustice.

This isn't the only time Solomon makes a case for our direct involvement in social injustice:

> Open your mouth for the mute,
> For the rights of all the unfortunate.
> Open your mouth, judge righteously,
> And defend the rights of the afflicted and needy.
> (Prov. 31:8–9)

Are the unborn mute? Can they speak for themselves? Is a young mother being coerced to abort her baby someone we should assist and defend? Is a child in the womb about to be aborted a person we consider afflicted and needy?

Perhaps the most powerful and poignant Old Testament story about our obligation to protect life comes from Exodus 1. Recall that Joseph became second-in-command of Egypt and rescued his family from the famine that was coming to the land. As a result, the nation of Israel grew and flourished inside Egypt. By the time we reach Exodus 1, Joseph is long gone, and Israel has grown into a large people in a foreign land. A new king of Egypt arrives, and he feels threatened by the size of the Israelite population.

His solution to his perceived problem? Male population control. Although he eventually takes a more direct approach, his first attempt to control the male birth rate of Israel is to compel the Hebrew midwives to do his deadly, dirty work for him:

> Then the king of Egypt spoke to the Hebrew midwives, one of whom was named Shiphrah and the other was named Puah; and he said, "When you are helping the Hebrew women to give birth and see them upon the birthstool, if it is a son, then you shall put him to death; but if it is a daughter, then she shall live." But the midwives feared God, and did not do as the king of Egypt had commanded them, but let the boys live.
>
> So the king of Egypt called for the midwives and said to them, "Why have you done this thing, and let the boys live?" The midwives said to Pharaoh, "Because the Hebrew women are not as the Egyptian women; for they are vigorous and give birth before the midwife can get to them." So God was good to the midwives, and the people multiplied, and became very mighty. Because the midwives feared God, He established households for them. (Exod. 1:15–21)

This passage is fascinating. The midwives are commanded to kill all male Hebrew babies. They ignore the command of the king, honoring God instead.

When Pharaoh discovers they haven't obeyed him, he calls them to account. The midwives appear to have devised a rather clever response to cover their tracks. They claim the Hebrew women are giving birth so fast they can't keep up. Perhaps the midwives lied, or perhaps they purposefully delayed their response to Hebrew women about to give birth. Either way, their refusal to murder the baby boys was a courageous and potentially deadly decision.

Does God condemn the midwives for their deception? Does He scold them for disobeying their government's (Pharaoh's) laws? Does He discourage their actions because they weren't submissive to civil authority?

On the contrary, God honors them. He is "good" to them. And He rewards the midwives by providing households for them. It may have been that these women were midwives because they couldn't have children of their own. Because of their faith and action, God provided them families.

God is the Author of Life. Not only does He command us *not* to take innocent life, He commands us to *protect* innocent life. And we honor Him when we do so.

The New Testament builds upon the law and commands of the Old Testament. Christ, as the fulfillment of the Old Testament law, challenges us even further with a comprehensive application of its principles. When a scribe pressed Jesus to rank the law and commandments, His answer has provided simple guidance to us ever since:

> Jesus answered, "The foremost is, 'Hear, O Israel! The Lord our God is one Lord; and you shall love the Lord your God with all your heart, and with all your soul, and with all your mind, and with all your strength.' The second is this, 'You shall love your neighbor as yourself.' There is no other commandment greater than these." (Mark 12:29–31)

129

Love God. Love your neighbor as yourself.

Is the unborn our neighbor? Is the family at risk to abort our neighbor? Is the post-abortive man and woman our neighbor? Who exactly is our neighbor, and what is our obligation to him or her?

The parable of the good Samaritan answers the question. A snarky lawyer asked Jesus to clarify whom He meant by "neighbor." Jesus gave him an unexpected reply:

> "A man was going down from Jerusalem to Jericho, and fell among robbers, and they stripped him and beat him, and went away leaving him half dead. And by chance a priest was going down on that road, and when he saw him, he passed by on the other side. Likewise a Levite also, when he came to the place and saw him, passed by on the other side.
>
> "But a Samaritan, who was on a journey, came upon him; and when he saw him, he felt compassion, and came to him and bandaged up his wounds, pouring oil and wine on them; and he put him on his own beast, and brought him to an inn and took care of him. On the next day he took out two denarii and gave them to the innkeeper and said, 'Take care of him; and whatever more you spend, when I return I will repay you.'
>
> "Which of these three do you think proved to be a neighbor to the man who fell into the robbers' hands?" And he said, "The one who showed mercy toward him." Then Jesus said to him, "Go and do the same." (Luke 10:30–37)

In our culture of abortion-riddled death, this passage should weigh on us like a ton of bricks. Note that the first two people to ignore the half-dead man were religious leaders. The priests were the teachers of the day, and a Levite was a member of the tribe of Levi, the group of the Israelites responsible for the temple and religious observances.

They were respected members of the church and men who should have embodied compassion and mercy. Yet they ignored the plight of the beaten man.

The Samaritan man came to the victim's rescue. Not only did he physically help the man to safety, he provided financially for him and made arrangements for his long-term care. Samaritans were half-breed outcasts to Jews. It was insulting to the lawyer that Jesus would use a Samaritan as a godly example. Yet Jesus, always challenging the prejudices and racism of the day, pointed to the heart as the true indicator of a person's worth, not the race or religious background.

It's interesting to note that Jesus never directly answered the lawyer's question. The lawyer had asked him, "Who is my neighbor?" In other words, he wanted to know whom he was obligated to love. Was it just Jews? Was it people of a certain class, race, or gender? Was it people who lived near him or whom he interacted with on a daily basis? The passage notes the lawyer wanted to justify himself. He wanted to check to see if he was being neighborly to the right type of people.

But Jesus doesn't tell the lawyer who his neighbor is. He finishes the story and then turns the question around on the lawyer: "Which of these three do you think proved to be a neighbor to the man who fell into the robbers' hands?" Jesus is not telling the lawyer he should be a neighbor to Samaritans. Jesus uses the Samaritan, the outcast, the racially profiled, the reject of society, to point out the sin in the lawyer's question. The Samaritan embodies the heart of a neighbor, and He shows the lawyer the answer is not one of location or class. He is once again pointing to the heart, not external circumstances or characteristics.

Who then is our neighbor? If we are to be like the Samaritan, the answer is anyone in our path who is hurting or in trouble. We are to ignore race, gender, color, social status, or prejudices.

Are the unborn and their families our neighbors? If they are hurting, in trouble, or in need of practical help, they are indeed our neighbors. And Jesus is clear—we are to step in and help.

Jesus emphasizes the same point in the Sermon on the Mount:

> Ask, and it will be given to you; seek, and you will find; knock, and it will be opened to you. For everyone who asks receives, and he who seeks finds, and to him who knocks it will be opened. Or what man is there among you who, when his son asks for a loaf, will give him a stone? Or if he asks for a fish, he will not give him a snake, will he? If you then, being evil, know how to give good gifts to your children, how much more will your Father who is in heaven give what is good to those who ask Him! In everything, therefore, treat people the same way you want them to treat you, for this is the Law and the Prophets. (Matt. 7:7–12)

Treat others the way you want to be treated. This Golden Rule has served as a core basis of Western law for hundreds of years.

We are then obligated to treat the unborn the way we want to be treated. We are to treat at-risk parents the same. Do we wish to be ripped limb from limb, drawn and quartered because we were conceived? Of course not. Do we wish to experience judgment, derision, or neglect because we made the decision to abort a child somewhere in our past? We don't want to be treated that way. Do we want to be coerced to take the life of a child because the child is inconvenient or unplanned? Do we want to be manipulated and lied to under fear of rejection? Many women facing abortion feel that way. No, that is not treating our neighbor as ourselves.

If you still find yourself questioning whether or not children (born or unborn) are precious neighbors of the church, consider Jesus's words:

> At that time the disciples came to Jesus and said, "Who then is greatest in the kingdom of heaven?" And He called a child to Himself and set him before them, and said, "Truly I say to you, unless you are converted and become like children, you will not enter the kingdom of heaven. Whoever then humbles himself as this child, he is the greatest in the kingdom of heaven. And whoever receives one such child in My name receives Me; but whoever causes one of these little ones who believe in Me to stumble, it would be better for him to have a heavy millstone hung around his neck, and to be drowned in the depth of the sea." (Matt. 18:1–6)

The Bible in both testaments, whether through negative or positive commands, is crystal clear that the church, God's people, is to be actively engaged in protecting and rescuing the innocent, lost, and victimized people in our community. We are not to discriminate. Man, woman, black, white, straight, gay, handicapped, lost, born or unborn, the Christian church is commanded and called to restore, redeem, heal, shelter, and rescue. We are to reconcile what is broken for the glory of our God.

The unborn represent the most innocent, voiceless, and weakest among us. They and their families deserve our utmost efforts, not our silence or ignorance.

We are without excuse.

PART 3
Ending Abortion in America

The Confused Church

"O ur belief in the sanctity of unborn human life makes us reluctant to approve abortion," declares one prominent church body. "But we are equally bound to respect the sacredness of the life and well-being of the mother and the unborn child.

"We recognize tragic conflicts of life with life that may justify abortion, and in such cases we support the legal option of abortion under proper medical procedures by certified medical providers."[129]

This is not the position statement of a public educational institution, a government entity, or a pro-abortion organization. It is the official position of the United Methodist Church.

Tragically, the United Methodist Church's pro-abortion position was a driving force in the passage of *Roe v. Wade*, the Supreme Court decision that ushered America into the abortion age. Supreme Court Justice Harry Blackmun, who wrote the controversial abortion ruling, was an active United Methodist layman until his 1999 death at age ninety. Sarah Weddington, the lead attorney for the abortion cause in *Roe*, is the daughter of a Methodist minister.

Weddington took up the abortion cause in part out of a misguided desire to help others. She cites the influence of her father, who was not a "fire-and-brimstone variety" preacher, but one whose "focus was the gospel of 'Christian social concern' that we as Christians have a responsibility to look beyond our individual lives and act out of a concern for others." In reaching her decision to challenge the Texas abortion law, Weddington apparently also took moral guidance from the United Methodist Church, which she notes had "publicly stated its opposition to laws making abortion a crime,"[130] a stance adopted in 1970.

Though the Roman Catholic Church has been a clear and uncompromised voice for life, when it comes to Protestantism, it's a different story. For the most part, the shepherds of the flock—both liberal and conservative—have been on the wrong side of the abortion debate or have kept silent since the 1960s.

The theological leftward drift of some of America's mainline churches—think Methodists, Presbyterians, Episcopalians, and the United Church of Christ—is a well-known story. So it may not surprise you to learn that some of these church bodies were early advocates of easy abortion and that they still support the right to take the life of voiceless boys and girls.

It is little wonder that the Christian church in America doesn't defend and protect the unborn when large denominations support child sacrifice. These denominations have rejected much of the Bible, hundreds of years of clear teaching, and their own calling to protect life in order to conform to society's acceptance of the practice. They preach a form of love and compassion while quietly nodding in assent when millions of the youngest human beings are slaughtered in the womb. It is deadly hypocrisy and a clear offense to the gospel.

If the church, in its entirety, is to rise up and cooperatively work to end abortion in America, we must first examine the reasons behind our silence. This chapter focuses on the historical chaos in the Protestant church regarding abortion, and that confusion is instructive. We can't work together to end abortion unless we agree that it is morally, biblically wrong, and as this chapter shows, we have a long way to go to reach that correct consensus. History proves that even conservative evangelicals have been muddled at best on their abortion views.

In the following chapters, I take a long, hard look at the doctrinal positions of major denominations or groups on the sacredness of human life and compare them with the three-part biblical apologetic. Then I present a simple blueprint for any church, regardless of denomination or sect, to lovingly, compassionately, and truthfully get involved in the effort to stop the killing of our children.

We do not have to accept abortion as a future reality. But first we must understand how we reached this point.

A History of Confusion

The history of the American church and the abortion holocaust shows a clear divide: liberal Protestant churches who were pro-abortion and worked for its legalization, and evangelical leaders who were confused or misinformed.

The American Baptist Convention was the first major mainline church to come out with a pro-abortion resolution when it announced in 1968 that "abortion should be a matter of responsible, personal decision" legally available up to the twelfth week.[131] In 1970, the United Methodist General Conference issued its first official position on abortion when it passed a resolution addressing the "population crisis," declaring that states should "remove the regulation of abortion from the criminal code."[132] The United Church of Christ called in 1971 for the "repeal of all legal prohibitions of physician-performed abortions" to "make voluntary and medically safe abortions legally available to all women."[133] The United Presbyterian Church, USA endorsed "full free-dom of personal choice" for women in 1972.[134] That was a 180-degree swing from ten years earlier when the church reaffirmed its historic and unequivocally pro-life position, stating, "The fetus is a human life to be protected by the criminal law from the moment when the ovum is fertilized."[135]

Just for historical reference, here is what the Presbyterian Church said in 1869 in one of the most unambiguous and forceful pro-life statements I have ever encountered:

> This Assembly regards the destruction by parents of their own offspring, before birth, with abhorrence, as a crime against God and against nature; and as the frequency of such murders can no longer be concealed, we hereby warn those that are guilty of this crime that, except they repent, they cannot inherit eternal life. We also exhort those who have been called to preach the gospel, and all who love purity and the truth, and who would avert the just judgments of Almighty God from the nation, that they be no longer silent, or tolerant of these things, but that they endeavour by all proper means to stay the floods of impurity and cruelty.[136]

One hundred years later, mainline church bodies called on the US Supreme Court to legalize abortion. The United Church of Christ, along with branches of the Episcopal Church, USA and the United Methodist Church, joined a "friend of the court" brief urging the Court to strike down laws criminalizing abortion in Texas and Georgia in the *Roe v. Wade* case.

In 1967, a liberal minister in New York's Greenwich Village co-founded an abortion referral service that was counseling some 150,000 women a year in twenty-six states just three years later.[137] Rev. Howard Moody's Clergy Consultation Service on Abortion enlisted the aid of some 1,400 Protestant ministers and Jewish rabbis to steer pregnant women to doctors willing to do illegal abortions.[138] Moody, pastor of Judson Memorial Church, which is affiliated with the American Baptist Churches and the United Church of Christ, also helped found a New York City abortion clinic in 1970, which was led for a time by Dr. Bernard Nathanson and which became the largest abortion clinic in the world. In 1973, Moody's pro-abortion clergy network and other factions within liberal denominations founded the Religious Coalition for Abortion Rights, renamed the Religious Coalition for Reproductive Choice in 1993.

What may surprise you is that while Moody and company were helping women get illegal abortions, some evangelical leaders and churches also supported abortion legalization. Just when unborn children most needed advocates with spiritual and moral authority, the evangelical church was confused and compromised in its response to the pro-abortion cause.

Christianity Today, the flagship publication of American evangelicalism, along with the Christian Medical Society, gathered twenty-five theological, medical, and legal experts in 1968 for a four-day symposium to address contraception, abortion, and sterilization. The "Protestant Symposium on the Control of Human Reproduction" convened practicing physicians; academics in the fields of sociology, psychiatry, and genetics; representatives from Dallas, Trinity, Gordon (later Gordon-Conwell), Northern Baptist, and Fuller theological seminaries; and a former US Supreme Court justice. These experts looked at abortion from legal, medical, and biblical perspectives and

141

arrived at conclusions in almost complete harmony with what the advocates of abortion legalization were proclaiming in the late 1960s.

"Whether or not the performance of an induced abortion is sinful we are not agreed, but about the necessity and permissibility for it under certain circumstances we are in accord," the doctors, scholars, and theologians at the symposium announced.[139] Their joint manifesto acknowledged, "The sanctity of life must be considered when the question of abortion is raised." At the same time, there also may be "compelling reasons why abortion must be considered under certain circumstances."[140] Those reasons included rape, incest, fetal defects, as well as the health and life of the mother—all valid indications for abortion according to a 1968 statement from the American College of Obstetricians and Gynecologists (ACOG) that was endorsed in full by the *Christianity Today*-Christian Medical Society symposium.

Symposium participants stipulated that they did not read the ACOG pronouncement as authorizing abortion on demand, but the doctors' group listed "health" concerns as a justification for abortion. In assessing the "risk to health," ACOG said "account may be taken of the patient's total environment, actual or reasonably foreseeable."[141] That's a vague and broadly worded formulation that still undergirds the ambiguous "health of the mother" justification for abortion today.

In what may be its most jarring, unscientific, and unbiblical assertion, symposium participants said it is only at "the moment of birth" that "the infant is a human being with all the rights which Scripture accords to all human beings."[142] Before birth, as symposium participant Dr. Bruce Waltke concluded, "the Old Testament does not equate the fetus with a living person."[143] Waltke substantially revised his view and adopted a pro-life position seven years later.[144] Nonetheless, his position "strongly influenced the thinking of a number of Symposium participants," according to John Warwick Montgomery, a pro-life scholar who attended the symposium and contributed a paper titled "The Christian View of the Fetus."[145]

And all this was not done in a political vacuum. The six-hundred-page published version of the symposium proceedings came out in early 1969 and included an editorial note telling readers that the position adopted by these evangelical leaders was "being presented to a state legislative committee charged with studying and proposing changes in the abortion laws of that state."[146] In his 2003 review of the early evangelical response to abortion, Russell D. Moore stated, "With such ambiguity even among conservative evangelicals, it is not difficult to see why American culture evolved to the point of accepting *Roe v. Wade* without a sense of overwhelming outrage."[147]

The views of the experts at the *Christianity Today*-Christian Medical Society inquiry into abortion were also adopted by other evangelical bodies. In 1971, the National Association of Evangelicals (NAE) affirmed its belief that "all life is a gift of God, so that neither the life of the unborn child nor the mother may be lightly taken." At the same time, the evangelical body recognized the "necessity for therapeutic abortions to safeguard the health or the life of the mother," leaving "health" undefined. The NAE, which now claims to represent some forty-five thousand churches in forty denominations, also said pregnancies from rape or incest "may require deliberate termination" after "psychological and religious counseling."[148] Two years later, the NAE issued a harsh rebuke of the Supreme Court's 1973 *Roe v. Wade* decision but also reaffirmed its prior support for "therapeutic abortion to safeguard the health or the life of the mother."[149]

The Southern Baptist Convention (SBC) embraced abortion rights in 1971 when it called on Southern Baptists to work for legislation that will allow the possibility of abortion under such conditions as rape, incest, clear evidence of severe fetal deformity, and carefully ascertained evidence of the likelihood of damage to the emotional, mental, and physical health of the mother.[150]

The SBC did not fully reverse course until 1980, when it endorsed a human life amendment to the US Constitution that would prohibit abortion except to save the life of the mother. Today the SBC is one of the few prominent pro-life Protestant religious groups.

W. A. Criswell, the long-time pastor of First Baptist Church of Dallas and a former president of the SBC, initially agreed with the Supreme Court's decision in *Roe*. Criswell's support stemmed from his view of the distinction between soul and body: "I have always felt that it was only after a child was born and had life separate from its mother that it became an individual person, and it has always, therefore, seemed to me that what is best for the mother and for the future should be allowed."[151] Like the denomination to which he belonged, Criswell later took up a solidly pro-life stance.

Popular evangelical philosopher and theologian Norman L. Geisler told readers in 1971 that "abortion is not necessarily murder" and may be justified to protect the mother, avoid giving birth to lives that will be "subhuman," and because of rape or incest.[152] "The rights to life, health, and self-determination—i.e., the rights to personhood—of the fully human mother take precedence over that of the potentially human embryo,"[153] Geisler explained. Like Waltke and Criswell, Geisler later reversed himself and joined the life-affirming community.

To its credit, *Christianity Today* denounced *Roe* in 1973 as a "pagan ruling," but a widespread evangelical mobilization against the ruling did not materialize. *Roe* provoked little outcry from the evangelical camp for almost six years, writes Cynthia Gorney, author of a five-hundred-page account of the recent history of abortion in America. "No great chorus of protest against *Roe* rose from the National Association of Evangelicals' member churches," Gorney informs. "Evangelical radio and television ministries kept their distance."[154]

Shortly after the US Supreme Court announced its 1973 abortion ruling, conservative Christian radio broadcaster Richard Bott interviewed a doctor who had campaigned for abortion legalization. The doctor made a vigorous case for legal abortion and *Roe*, after which Bott told his listeners to ponder his guest's points. "I remember telling the audience: 'You see, folks, it's a matter of opinion,'" Bott recalled. "'Some are very opposed to it. Others are of the opinion of Dr. Kranz. So you see, people have to make up their own minds.'"[155]

Forty years later, Dick Bott, with his son, Rich, operates a ninety station radio empire and is anything but ambivalent or ill-informed on abortion. Like many evangelicals, his initial confusion in the wake of *Roe* has been replaced with staunch support for the unborn—and for legal action to fix that support into law.

Even Billy Graham shrank from the pro-life cause in the 1970s, according to theologian and author Harold O. J. Brown. Graham, the nation's most popular and beloved evangelical leader, helped Brown and C. Everett Koop in 1975 launch the Christian Action Council, a pro-life evangelical group that later became CareNet, which supports some 1,100 affiliated crisis pregnancy centers across North America. Graham's initial backing included "a willingness to address the National Right to Life Committee," and his wife, Ruth, became a Christian Action Council sponsor. But that assistance quickly withered, Brown recalled:

Soon, however, warned off, it would seem, by the late Harriet Pilpel, his attorney at the time and a prominent strategist of the abortion movement, Graham dropped all support and his wife withdrew as a sponsor.[156]

Widespread evangelical opposition to abortion did not emerge until 1979. A crucial factor was a book and film series called *Whatever Happened to the Human Race* that was produced by Christian philosopher Francis Schaeffer and C. Everett Koop, the chief surgeon at Children's Hospital of Philadelphia. Koop recalled in his autobiography that the purpose of the project, which included a twenty-city tour in late 1979, was to "awaken the evangelical world—and anyone else who would listen—to the Christian imperative to do something to reverse the perilous realignment of American values on these life-and-death issues."[157]

However, response to *Whatever Happened* was mixed. "People went out from those seminars and there was a change," Schaeffer recalled in 1981. "Prior to that, to our shame, across the United States and Great Britain as well, there were very, very few evangelicals involved in the movement against abortion." Even so, the turnout at the seminars was sometimes sparse, Schaeffer wrote, due to the fact that "much of the evangelical leadership did not want to become involved."[158]

Obviously there was initial and substantial confusion among Christian leaders about abortion. Perhaps it was due to ignorance of medical facts, or perhaps it was because of theological murkiness. Whatever the cause, several denominations were heavily involved in the legalization of abortion, and other Christian leaders were unable to reach clarity in their views until years after the dam of *Roe v. Wade* was long broken.

CHAPTER 8
Deadly Doctrine

The Religious Coalition for Reproductive Choice (RCRC), an alliance of some forty religious organizations, published a pamphlet called "Considering Abortion? Clarifying What You Believe." The pamphlet proclaims, "You are to claim your godlike, God-given role in creation by saying yes or no, secure in the knowledge that whatever you decide, after having honestly sought what is right, God will bless."[159] They also claim, "Abortion is a divinely blessed and guided act that can be practiced by a sovereign, isolated moral agent without regard to any external moral or legal restraints and without concern about the moral status of the target of the act."[160]

Lest you think the RCRC is some kooky group of fringe churches, consider some of their member organizations: the United Methodist Church, the United Church of Christ, the Episcopal Church, the American Jewish Congress, and the Presbyterian Mission Agency. There are numerous mainstream denominations and churches affiliated with the RCRC.

The doctrine of the RCRC is based on their view that abortion is a "divinely blessed and guided act." Although the term "doctrine" is often derided as traditional, stodgy, or outdated, the underlying concept is actually fundamental to every person's worldview. Doctrine is simply a belief or set of beliefs held and taught by a church, political party, or other group.[161]

Each one of us holds to some sort of doctrine because each of us holds to a belief system. Our personal views about abortion are driven from some form of doctrine, whether it is based on our experience, our church, religious texts, someone else's influence, etc. Religious doctrine is therefore extremely relevant, and bad doctrine can be deadly.

Though the evangelical church was initially confused and probably uninformed about the abortion issue, the last chapter's brief look at recent history shows that numerous leaders and religious groups became solidly, biblically pro-life in time. So what about today? Are the overwhelming majority of American churches, who claim to follow Christ and adhere to the Bible, firmly against the abortion epidemic after forty years of theological study, ultrasound technology showing the mysteries of life in the womb, and moral debate? Are they teaching the basic principles of our faith and reinforcing the fact that God is our Creator and that He ordains all life?

To answer those questions, I asked our research team at Online for Life to investigate what American churches doctrinally confess concerning the sanctity of human life. Most of our research centered on Protestant denominations. The Roman Catholic Church, with 68.5 million members in the US, has historically been very clear about its unequivocal stance. Though I've noted Catholics in America often seem divided on the issue, the church itself is doctrinally pro-life without apology.

For our research project, we selected all major Protestant denominations or groups that reported having over 250,000 members (see www.DeliverUsFromAbortion.com for the complete study). Those churches report a combined total of almost seventy million members in the US. We then researched each denomination's doctrinal statements for official positions on the sanctity of human life and abortion.

A few notes:

- My own experience suggests that many nondenominational churches are pro-life. Because they are not linked into a larger group or denomination, they were not included in this study. The Calvary Chapel movement, for example, includes some 1,500 churches worldwide. Though the churches represent a large number of people and hold to certain specific doctrines, they are not a denomination.

- The nondenominational and Bible churches across the country are a vital part of the American church; however, we didn't have the data to be able to include them in our research.

- Some denominations have taken a "blended" doctrinal position. They acknowledge that God is the author and creator of life, and they believe life is sacred. At first glance they appear to be pro-life churches. However, these blended statements make exceptions and considerations for various circumstances and do not represent a biblical definition of the sacredness of human life. If a church provided an exception for abortion apart from saving the life of the mother, we placed them in the pro-abortion category. Since most of these "ride the fence" churches provide exceptions for the mental and physical health of the mother, they are using the same language and justification the abortion industry has used for decades.

- It may seem like a harsh distinction, as it appears these "ride the fence" denominations have legitimately wrestled with the issue. As I note below, several denominations have rather long, windy, flowery discourses in their statements about the sacredness of life, the difficulties of unplanned pregnancies, and the compassion and care that we need to extend to mothers in crisis pregnancies. Then they proceed to list all of the circumstances under which ripping a child limb from limb in the womb is acceptable. As we've discovered biblically, however, there is no gray area for abortion. You either view every life as sacred or you don't. To devalue human life based on arbitrary circumstances is to discriminate against what God Himself has created.

- Not all members of a pro-life denomination hold to those views, and not all churches affirm the pro-life worldview of their denominations. Conversely, not all churches in noncommittal or pro-abortion denominations hold to those views. And not all members of pro-abortion churches are pro-abortion. I know and work with numerous Methodists, for example, who are pro-life and are highly discouraged by the United Methodist Church's longstanding support for abortion.

- While our team made every attempt to articulate and separate denominations into various categories, it is not an exact science. Some denominations and groups blend into others (some groups roll up into others, some churches are part of more than one major group, etc.). Our conclusions are therefore general in nature. My intent is to paint the picture of abortion in the American church in broad strokes while understanding there are some nuances and irregularities in the source information.

Of the twenty-eight Protestant groups with over 250,000 members that we surveyed, seventeen have published an official position in their doctrinal documents. Of those that published a statement, nine are pro-life and eight are pro-abortion. We called the remaining eleven and asked them to provide their official position over the phone if available. Three responded that they are pro-life. The remaining eight did not return our repeated phone calls and inquiries.

So of these twenty-eight Protestant church bodies, twelve claim to be pro-life, eight are pro-abortion, and eight are unknown. The twelve groups that are pro-life account for thirty-two million members, around 47 percent of the total US Protestant population. Those denominations that support abortion rights represent over twenty million members. The eight silent denominations account for another 15.5 million members.

Protestant Church Members

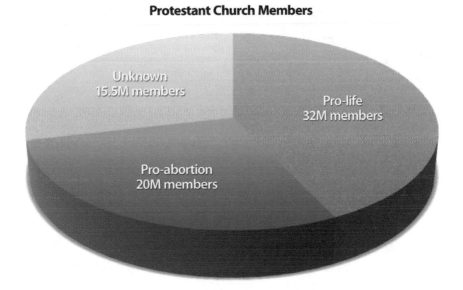

In short, about 53 percent of Protestants are members of religious groups that are not doctrinally pro-life by their admission or silence.

The Church of Jesus Christ of Latter-day Saints (Mormons), who claim six million members in the United States, are often regarded as pro-life, though the doctrinal statement on their website makes several exceptions. It allows for abortion consideration in cases of rape, incest, life of the mother, and potentially fatal prenatal conditions. Therefore their doctrinal statement is in conflict with a biblically based pro-life view. Jewish congregations, who also represent six million members, are generally pro-abortion (there are minor exceptions depending on the branch of Judaism). We were unable to locate a doctrinal statement on abortion for the Eastern Orthodox churches, consisting of some 3.7 million members. The Greek Orthodox Church does provide a statement, and they are biblically pro-life.

Seven African-American denominations qualified for the study. Two are pro-life (Church of God in Christ and Pentecostal Assemblies of the World) and the other five wouldn't return our calls. Total membership in these seven denominations is over twenty-one million people. The pro-life groups represent seven million people, so the majority of black church members may well be attending pro-abortion or silent churches.

If we lump together all sects, groups, and denominations, around 108 million people are part of churches that are doctrinally pro-life. Catholics account for almost two-thirds of that entire population. With some 108 million members in denominations that claim to be pro-life, we would expect to find far more Christians who are passionate about protecting the unborn. Perhaps the primary reason the pro-life doctrine isn't adopted by its members is because the doctrine isn't taught.

Silence of the Lambs

In 1994, *World* magazine published a groundbreaking article detailing the silence of evangelical pastors in relation to the abortion holocaust.

Indicative of the mood of the time, the article reported Billy Graham's belief that addressing abortion in the pulpit could impede his "main message" of salvation. "I don't get into these things like abortion," Graham told talk show host Larry King.

Authors Joe Maxwell and Steve Hall, authors of that original study in *World*, decided to refresh their study in January 2014. Their conclusion? Not much has changed. In addition to a survey Maxwell and Hall conducted that validated their concern, they noted the general tone in the pro-life movement:

> 25 national pro-life leaders—both evangelicals and Roman Catholics—gathered recently in Washington, D.C., in a meeting organized by National March for Life. Members of the group complained that many evangelical pastors are dropping the ball. "One of our great frustrations has been the silence of the evangelical pastors," said Sherry Crater, coalitions liaison at the Family Research Council.

I was one of the twenty-five leaders at this meeting. There was consensus among the others that, while Catholic leaders are often eager and willing to discuss the abortion epidemic, Protestant leaders are far less likely to do so.

Maxwell and Hall cite four primary reasons for the reluctance:

1. Preaching on the issue might discomfort church members or hurt women in congregations who've had abortions.
2. Preaching on the issue should not be done as a one-note tune or "hobby-horse," especially if the pastor emphasizes expository preaching.

3. Preaching on the issue might politically stigmatize the pastor or politicize the pulpit, scaring seekers off.

4. Preaching on the issue might seem uncool or anti-intellectual.[162]

God forbid we preach on something that has impacted tens of millions of parents and resulted in fifty-six million deaths. That would be uncool.

Deadly Doctrine

Silence from so many evangelical leaders and groups helps explain why the abortion holocaust isn't front and center among many conservative Christians. A brief look at pro-abortion church doctrinal statements certainly explains their silence or active promotion of the abortion holocaust.

Let's start with a simple, biblically based doctrinal statement about the sacredness of human life. The Southern Baptist Convention provides this clear commentary:

> Procreation is a gift from God, a precious trust reserved for marriage. At the moment of conception, a new being enters the universe, a human being, a being created in God's image. This human being deserves our protection, whatever the circumstances of conception.[163]

The Assemblies of God is likewise direct and to the point:

> The Assemblies of God views the practice of abortion as an evil that has been inflicted upon millions of innocent babies and that will threaten millions more in

the years to come. Abortion is a morally unacceptable alternative for birth control, population control, sex selection, and elimination of the physically and mentally handicapped. . . .The Scriptures regularly treat the unborn child as a person under the care of God.

Churches committed to abortion rights may also take a simple approach:

The United Church of Christ has affirmed and re-affirmed since 1971 that access to safe and legal abortion is consistent with a woman's right to follow the dictates of her own faith and beliefs in determining when and if she should have children, and it has supported comprehensive sexuality education as one measure to prevent unwanted or unplanned pregnancies, and to create healthy and responsible sexual persons and relationships.[164]

Let's compare this statement with our three-part, life-affirming apologetic:
1. God is the author of all life.
2. God does not permit mankind to kill innocent life.
3. The church is called to protect innocent life.

Since the statement doesn't mention the Creator, allows women to define their own faith, and doesn't even attempt to preserve unborn life under any circumstances, we can rest assured the United Church of Christ is anti-biblical on this point.

Let's look at some more creative doctrinal statements that attempt to "ride the fence." These types of doctrinal positions are usually long-winded and attempt to position the church on both sides. On one hand, they want to affirm life and the Creator. On the other hand, they want to avoid offending their pro-abortion constituents.

Presbyterian Church, USA

Under the heading "Areas of Substantial Agreement on the Issue of Abortion," the Presbyterian Church, USA (PCUSA) notes the following:

> Problem pregnancies are the result of, and influenced by, so many complicated and insolvable circumstances that we have neither the wisdom nor the authority to address or decide each situation.
>
> We affirm the ability and responsibility of women, guided by the Scriptures and the Holy Spirit, in the context of their communities of faith, to make good moral choices in regard to problem pregnancies.
>
> . . . The considered decision of a woman to terminate a pregnancy can be a morally acceptable, though certainly not the only or required, decision. Possible justifying circumstances would include medical indications of severe physical or mental deformity, conception as a result of rape or incest, or conditions under which the physical or mental health of either woman or child would be gravely threatened.
>
> . . . We are disturbed by abortions that seem to be elected only as a convenience or to ease embarrassment.

We affirm that abortion should not be used as a method of birth control.

Abortion is not morally acceptable for gender selection only or solely to obtain fetal parts for transplantation.

The strong Christian presumption is that since all life is precious to God, we are to preserve and protect it. Abortion ought to be an option of last resort.[165]

It's interesting to note that while the PCUSA acknowledges it doesn't have "the wisdom or authority" to address various crisis pregnancy situations, it apparently does feel it has the wisdom and authority to condone killing unborn children.

Let's run this through our three-part test.

1. God is the author of all life: the PCUSA confirms that all life is precious to God. Yet they then acknowledge we can kill innocent life as a last resort. If all life is precious to God, why is there a "last resort" that puts us in a position to play God?

2. Man does not have the right to kill innocent life: the PCUSA is a master of equivocation on this point. While they bemoan abortion for birth control or gender selection, they affirm that abortion may be appropriate for other circumstances, including the all-ambiguous "health of the mother." Here the PCUSA ignores that God continually works through trial, tribulation, suffering, and adverse circumstances for His own Glory. And the creation of a new human being, made in the image of God, is a blessing, not a curse.

3. The church is called to protect life: the irony is inescapable. They affirm the church should protect life and, at the same

time, allow church members to kill life under numerous circumstances.

This is a statement intended not to offend anybody. It is also a statement intended not to protect anybody, namely children. Ironically, a separate PCUSA social justice statement affirms the church's commitment to seek to abolish "the exploitation of children," but the unborn are excluded from the church's definition of "children."[166]

United Methodist Church

The United Methodist position would probably make John Wesley sick to his stomach. He was, after all, the fifteenth child in a poverty-stricken household. He may have been aborted had he been conceived in the United States today. Wesley writes:

> Our belief in the sanctity of unborn human life makes us reluctant to approve abortion. But we are equally bound to respect the sacredness of the life and well-being of the mother, for whom devastating damage may result from an unacceptable pregnancy. In continuity with past Christian teaching, we recognize tragic conflicts of life with life that may justify abortion, and in such cases we support the legal option of abortion under proper medical procedures. We cannot affirm abortion as an acceptable means of birth control, and we unconditionally reject it as a means of gender selection.
>
> . . . We call all Christians to a searching and prayerful inquiry into the sorts of conditions that may warrant abortion. [167]

The United Methodist Church has been an abortion proponent for decades, and their statement contradicts the clear teachings of the Bible.

1. God is the author of all life: like other lukewarm statements, the Methodist Church affirms the sanctity of human life. Though they don't explicitly say it, they seem to acknowledge all life is precious.

2. Man does not have the right to kill unborn life: according to the Methodists, yes we do, especially if the life is a weak, unseen, unborn, defenseless human being. They clearly value the life of the mother over the child and provide for the mother killing her child under the normal ambiguous circumstances. This is in direct contradiction with the scriptures, which make no distinction in value between the born and the unborn.

3. The church is called to protect life: while they are "reluctant" to approve abortion, they do so. This is in direct violation of Proverbs 24, which calls us to "deliver those being taken away to death."

Though they reject abortion as birth control, I previously noted that the United Methodist Church was a founding member of the Religious Coalition for Reproductive Choice, which has as its slogan "Pro-Faith, Pro-Family, Pro-Choice." RCRC leased space until 1993 in the United Methodist Building, a five-story structure across the street from the US Supreme Court and the US Capitol Building.

Holy Abortion?, a careful 1993 critique of RCRC, concluded that the organization "treats abortion as a holy, moral, liberating, empowering, divine gift and right." That stance is even more extreme than the pro-abortion position adopted by its Protestant members. *Holy Abortion?* authors Michael J. Gorman and Ann Loar Brooks note that "three of the four affiliated mainline Protestant churches—and even to some degree the fourth member (the United Church of Christ)—view abortion as a tragic last resort that should generally be avoided and cannot be easily condoned. This is a fundamental and indeed antithetical difference between the RCRC and the mainline Protestant churches."[168]

But nonetheless these churches (Methodists among them) remain tied to the RCRC.

The Salvation Army

When I was a boy, I was part of my local Kiwanis Boys Choir. One year our choir volunteered with the Salvation Army during the Christmas season. Each of us paired up with a bell-ringer outside of local grocery stores and encouraged shoppers to drop loose change into the famous red kettle. Our choir director decided to turn our volunteerism into a contest, and the boy who raised the most money in his respective kettle would be declared the winner.

I am unnaturally competitive, and at that age I was unnaturally short. So I decided to play the Tiny Tim card, donned puppy-dog eyes, and charmed shoppers (mostly older women) to turn over their change and, in some cases, whatever bills they had in their wallets. Sure enough, I handily beat the taller choir members. I was declared the winner and presented with a wonderful certificate. I couldn't have been prouder.

This is the image most of us associate with the Salvation Army: Christmas, bells, red kettles, and money being donated to a very worthy cause. The Salvation Army is one of the strongest, most secure brands in the entire United States, with good reason. They consistently minister to the poorest in our society, and they have a long and storied history of serving the destitute, downtrodden, and weak among us with compassion and faithfulness.

So when it came time to study the Salvation Army's position on abortion, I assumed their doctrine concerning the unborn would parallel their obvious commitment to the dignity and worth of born human beings. Yet the International Salvation Army counts itself among the conflicted denominations with a long and confusing position statement.

The "the official position of The Salvation Army," as stated on the Salvation Army International website, is the following:

> Abortion is defined as an operation or other procedure to terminate a pregnancy before the foetus is viable. . . .
>
> The Salvation Army believes all people are created in the image of God and therefore have unique and intrinsic value. Human life is sacred and all people should be treated with dignity and respect. The Salvation Army accepts the moment of fertilisation as the start of human life. . . .
>
> The Salvation Army believes that life is a gift from God and we are answerable to God for the taking of life. As such, The Salvation Army is concerned about the growing ready acceptance of abortion, which reflects insufficient concern for vulnerable persons including the unborn. We do not believe that genetic abnormalities that are identified in an unborn child who is likely to live longer than a brief period after birth are sufficient to warrant a termination of pregnancy.
>
> The Salvation Army recognizes tragic and perplexing circumstances that require difficult decisions regarding a pregnancy. . . .

The Salvation Army believes that termination can occur only when carrying the pregnancy further seriously threatens the life of the mother; or reliable diagnostic procedures have identified a foetal abnormality considered incompatible with survival for more than a very brief post natal period.

In addition, rape and incest are brutal acts of dominance violating women physically and emotionally. This situation represents a special case for the consideration of termination as the violation may be compounded by the continuation of the pregnancy.[169]

We should always be careful how we use words to describe abortion. The Salvation Army International intentionally avoids truthful language when it defines abortion as "an operation to terminate a pregnancy before a foetus is viable."

Abortion is the willful killing of an unborn human life. And abortions are entirely legal beyond "viability" in numerous states under the US Supreme Court's 1973 abortion rulings.

Let's put the statement to the test:

1. God is the author of all life: The Salvation Army affirms this in accordance with Scripture.

2. Mankind is not permitted to kill innocent life: here the Salvation Army goes to great lengths to permit abortion without offending. While claiming the value of human life is based on God, they equivocate by simultaneously claiming we can devalue human life under certain circumstances and kill lives that we deem less valuable. This includes fetal abnormality, rape, and incest. They provide no explanation why a baby conceived in

those circumstances loses her value, or why those lives are no longer "gifts from God."

3. The church is called to protect life: the Salvation Army only agrees if life meets their criteria. While the it claims we are answerable to God for taking life, we apparently only have to answer in some cases.

Episcopal Church and Evangelical Lutheran Church of America

Other groups such as the Episcopal Church and Evangelical Lutheran Church of America follow a similar formula:

1. All life is sacred and a gift from God.
2. They are "concerned" about abortion.
3. Abortion is acceptable for fetal deformity, rape, and incest.

Some also want to limit abortions prior to viability.

The primary challenge of virtually all of these statements is the stubborn and illogical demand to devalue the child based on situations we deem appropriate. Every human being, regardless of condition or circumstances of conception, is created in His image. Every unborn child is a masterful work of a creative God. Every child has priceless worth.

The dichotomy and hypocrisy is unmistakable. If a child is conceived into socially acceptable circumstances and is wanted, the child is ordained by God and has value. If the child is conceived through crime or suffers medical challenges, the child is apparently not ordained by God and loses value. And the child doesn't lose some value—the child is worthless. And the child is ripped up and thrown away, usually with no honor and no burial.

While the focus on the mother and extended family in difficult, if not tragic, circumstances is most certainly warranted, the complete

163

refusal to acknowledge the value of the unborn child as equal to the mother is unbiblical and unethical. Instead of forging doctrinal statements to appease various factions, churches should promote doctrine and practice that treats all humans as equals, and extends compassion, tangible, life-preserving care to all—not just some.

Leading from the Top?

There are most certainly heroic and effective efforts to end abortion happening in cities and towns across America. Thousands of individuals, parachurch organizations, and local churches are ministering to women in crisis, counseling men, providing tangible help and support, and working in their communities to communicate a loving, biblical worldview of the sacredness of human life. Some of these individuals and churches are part of pro-life denominations, and others are part of pro-abortion denominations. They all understand what's at stake.

At the same time, I can't help but wonder why the quest to end abortion isn't being reinforced at the national level of some pro-life denominations. Many large groups promote and drive national missions efforts, conferences, training programs, workshops, church-building initiatives, evangelism efforts, and public awareness campaigns.

Why aren't there more national denominational efforts to end abortion?

While I deeply appreciate those denominations and groups that promote and teach the sacredness of human life doctrinally, I would argue that we are hard pressed to find any other issue that deserves more attention from the top of denominational leadership.

Here's a sample of what a few pro-life denominations are (or aren't) doing from the top down.

The Evangelical Free Church of America

A church representative told us that the church does not have an official statement on abortion but does hold to the belief that life begins at conception. She affirmed that the association is pro-life and asserted that all of the denomination's churches hold that position.

At the same time, the 290,000-member denomination doesn't promote the pro-life perspective among its churches. The church representative said that since each church practices self-government, resources advancing the interests of the unborn are not provided by the church body's national leadership.

Presbyterian Church in America

The Presbyterian Church in America (PCA) was founded in 1973 and is one of those evangelical bodies that wasted little time in opposing abortion. The church, which now has 364,000 members, emphasized its biblical duty to address abortion, saying, "God in His Word speaks of the unborn child as a person and treats him as such, and so must we. The Bible teaches the sanctity of life, and so must we."[170]

Rev. Bob Hornick, the assistant to the stated clerk of the PCA General Assembly, told us that the PCA has no pro-life initiatives at the national level. Instead, local churches may pursue a variety of initiatives, including Sanctity of Human Life Sunday observances and fundraisers to help local unwed mothers and crisis pregnancy centers. Hornick said churches do "more than just holding up signs" and their ministry in the pro-life area "comes from the bottom, not the top."

Lutheran Church–Missouri Synod

The Lutheran Church-Missouri Synod (LCMS) has defended the unborn child from abortion in a series of resolutions since 1971.

Today, the conservative body of 2.3 million members remains true to its pro-life principles and matches its talk with an aggressive and comprehensive list of resources and programs to help churches engage in effective pro-life activity.

The LCMS is, to our knowledge, the only Protestant denomination with its own ministry dedicated to addressing the sanctity of human life. Maggie Karner, Director of Life Ministries for the LCMS, told us that she works with churches to help them understand how to live out the denomination's pro-life theology. She interacts with clergy in all thirty-five LCMS districts to provide education to pastors, congregations, and schools about life issues. She also ensures that all of the more than 170 Special Ministry Organizations associated with the LCMS are aligned with life issues.

The denominational website features a long list of pro-life resources at http://www.lcms.org/life, including a speakers bureau, information about a "Life Conference," "Life Sunday," and a well-stocked "Life Library" listing numerous helpful resources.

Assemblies of God

With three million adherents, the Assemblies of God (AG) is an "unashamedly pro-life" denomination and bases its view "on the biblical truth that all human life is created in the image of God (Genesis 1:27). From that truth issues the long-standing Christian view that aborting the life of a developing child is evil."

An AG spokeswoman told us that the church works with the Vitae Society, which uses outdoor advertising and video spots to advocate for life. She said local AG churches decide how, or if, they will observe the annual Sanctity of Human Life Sunday in January.

Church of God (Cleveland, Tenn.)

The Church of God (Cleveland, Tennessee) is a strongly pro-life church body of more than one million members. It addressed abortion in an unabashed 1976 statement that refers to abortion as "a vicious attack on the weakest and most helpless form of human life." In that same statement, the Pentecostal church asserted "that it is the duty of the church to raise an authoritative moral voice concerning this vital issue" and urged its "entire constituency to actively oppose any liberalization of abortion laws by state legislatures and by the Congress of the United States."[171]

The Church of God's list of "Practical Commitments" also exhorts members to "fulfill our obligations to society by being good citizens, by correcting social injustices, and by protecting the sanctity of life."[172]

Christian and Missionary Alliance

The Christian and Missionary Alliance (CMA) is a 425,000-member church body that stated in 1981 that "life begins at conception" and that "abortion on demand is morally wrong."[173]

Without providing specific detail, Mark Failing, an assistant to the president of the CMA, told us that pro-life work is taking place both formally and informally within the two-thousand-church denomination.

Church of the Nazarene

The 650,000-member Church of the Nazarene is fully pro-life and seeks to channel pro-life energy into practical aid to women and children. A statement on its website proclaims that

> [s]ince the inception of the practice of medical abortion, the Church of the Nazarene has expressed both its

sorrow and its strongest condemnation of the practice of aborting the unborn for the sake of convenience, ending unwanted pregnancies, or population control. As a denomination, our resolve has been strong in our struggle against this moral blight on the conscience of America.[174]

Specifically, this means "the initiation and support of programs designed to provide care for mothers and children." Such programs include "counseling centers, homes for expectant mothers, and the creation or utilization of Christian adoption services."

The church statement contends that "multitudes of Nazarene ministries and congregations are on the front lines providing ministries and interventions of 'responsible opposition to abortion.'" Such "proactive engagement," the church statement asserts, "transforms mere outrage to redemptive ministry in the name of Christ."[175]

Southern Baptist Convention

The SBC, as noted earlier, adopted a pro-abortion stance in 1971, but emerged in 1980 as an adamantly pro-life church body, calling for a Human Life Amendment to protect the unborn. Today the sixteen-million-member Protestant church has not budged an inch from its pro-life stance.

Bobby Reed, a vice president at the SBC Ethics and Religious Liberty Commission (ERLC), told us that the SBC is organized as a group of independent churches, not a religious hierarchy, a polity which gives individual churches freedom to differ with denominational statements. This freedom is apparently being exercised. A third of SBC members think abortion should be legal in all or most cases. Polling from Pew

Research shows that 36 percent of SBC members want abortion to be legal all or most of the time, while 59 percent think it should be illegal in all or most cases.[176]

However, the ERLC advocates in Washington for the unborn, as well as for religious liberty and other concerns. In addition, numerous resources are available to churches at SBC websites, including free bulletin inserts, a pro-life sermon, links to pro-life apologetics, and news about the pro-life movement.

As I've argued, abortion is primarily a spiritual issue. It is the willful, unjust killing of a human life—a life created by God and made in His image. For those churches, denominations, and groups who promote abortion vocally or silently, I urge you to change your view and your doctrinal position. Your active or passive acceptance of the abortion holocaust does great damage to the kingdom of God. If your church does not hold to the sacredness of human life from conception onward and does not believe that every life deserves protection, your church is quite simply wrong. And the incorrect or missing doctrine is deadly.

For those churches, denominations, and groups who are pro-life but not actively promoting that stance from the top levels of leadership, I must ask, "Why not?" Why does the senseless slaughter of millions of vulnerable children not have as high of a priority as church planting, evangelism, foreign missions, and polity?

Ask yourself this question: If Americans were killing 3,500 kindergartners every day, would your church or denomination work from the very top down to end the slaughter?

We are killing the same number of children every day—they are just younger than kindergartners. Let's get to work.

CHAPTER 9

Let the Church Arise:
Seven Steps to Ending Abortion

I haven't been able to rest since you told me about the abortion epidemic in our city and nation. I just had no idea we were losing so many babies. I didn't realize the impact on the family—every family! The amount of pain and suffering abortion has caused is virtually incalculable. What can we do? What can I do?"

A good friend of mine shared these words with me after I gave a short talk to a small group about the church's role in ending abortion. In our information-inundated society, many Christians have little idea of the abortion holocaust. Even if they have abortion in their past, they frequently bury their memories and repress their of guilt and shame in order to function.

In the case of abortion, ignorance in the church is not bliss. It's deadly.

This chapter provides a number of ways for the church to get engaged as it takes the lead in ending abortion in America. This is a role the church must take because the killing of millions of God's image-bearers requires the church's direct and aggressive involvement.

First, let's review some of the primary reasons many churches do not become directly involved with protecting innocent life and their families.

1.   Abortion is a "political issue."

A fellow employee at Online for Life, Ben, recently relayed a conversation he had with a staff member of a mega-church in the South. Ben began sharing about Online for Life, and the church staffer quickly tuned out.

"Our church doesn't deal with this issue," the staffer said. "It's too political."

Ben gently persisted and shared that, in addition to compassionately working with mothers at risk to abort, we also share messages of hope and healing for post-abortive parents.

The staff member softened a bit. "So this is about people? You are caring for people, not just about the politics?"

Ben replied in the affirmative. The church employee concluded, "Well, you'll never get your message in here if you talk about killing babies. But if you talk about healing, that might fly."

The church staffer's response would be silly if it wasn't so deadly. The church doesn't want to discuss the slaughter of innocent children because it's too political (yet something tells me they would discuss human trafficking, which also has numerous political implications). At least the staffer understood the importance of healing for post-abortive parents, though he prioritized it above the killing of human beings.

Though not all priests and parishes involve themselves in life-affirming efforts, the Catholic Church has been very clear on the spiritual underpinnings of abortion. Protestant churches, however, are often scared of preaching and teaching about abortion because, in their minds, abortion is primarily a political issue. Supposedly, if you are pro-life, you are Republican. If you are pro-choice, you are a Democrat. Because churches normally want to appear nonpolitical, they shy away from any issue that involves political controversy.

Paul Revere is probably rolling over in his grave. You need only do a brief survey of American church history to discover that Protestant churches were deeply committed to political activity. There was good reason "The Presbyterian Rebellion" was a nickname for the Revolutionary War. Christian churches were also key catalysts in the Underground Railroad and in the effort to end slavery.

America's independence and slavery could certainly be considered "political issues," and there was tremendous public conflict and disagreement over both. Yet numerous pastors were personally and publicly involved with both, and they worked tirelessly to glorify God by righting injustice.

Still, many of today's churches are content to avoid conflict, disagreement, or engagement in controversial subjects. In the *World* magazine article I cited earlier, the authors conducted an informal survey of forty pastors from seven member denominations in the National Association of Evangelicals. All said that life begins at conception, but eighteen pastors said they had not preached against abortion in the past year. Another five told *World* they had never addressed the topic from the pulpit. One reason pastors gave for not speaking out against abortion, *World* summarized, was that doing so "might politically stigmatize the pastor or politicize the pulpit, scaring seekers off."[177]

Abortion is avoided because we incorrectly accept it as a political football. According to Rev. Dean Nelson, a founding member of the National Pro-life Black Coalition, the erroneous politicization of abortion may be the primary reason many black churches remain silent. Because the majority of African-Americans are Democrat, they struggle with the tension of remaining loyal to a political party that, on the whole, supports abortion rights. So while many blacks are pro-life, to acknowledge so publicly would put them at odds with their political party.

But here's the bottom line: it is a lie from the pit of hell that abortion is primarily a political issue. It is a spiritual, moral issue with political aspects. Abortion is the willful killing of an unborn human being. Abortion is the result of a decision to snuff out the life of the weakest, most innocent of the human race.

It's not about polls, surveys, or votes. It's not about candidates, elections, reproductive rights, or empowerment. It is a person in a position of power taking the life of a person who has no power. When we allow abortion to become politicized, we diminish the severity of this holocaust, dishonor the children and families impacted by abortion, and place the responsibility of fixing the abortion problem on politicians and bureaucrats. But as the Bible clearly articulates, Christians are to be delivering those taken away to death and those staggering to slaughter.

Once we allow abortion to be politicized, it becomes impersonal. It becomes someone else's problem. It becomes a matter of public policy and Sunday morning talk shows. Instead of ministering to a woman with an unplanned pregnancy, instead of offering hope and forgiveness to a father consumed with guilt, instead of providing tangible help to a family in crisis, we cast a vote (or don't). We separate ourselves from taking personal responsibility to address the travesty of abortion and leave it to political operatives.

2. We don't want to offend anyone.

Pastors and priests are often reluctant to preach and teach about the sacredness of human life and abortion for fear of upsetting someone in their flock. They may be aware of pro-abortion members in their congregations, a key donor who has abortion in his or her past, or someone who is currently facing an unplanned pregnancy. While church leaders need to be sensitive to specific circumstances in their congregations, silence in the case of abortion is deadly. Would we rather not risk offending someone if it saves a human life?

Several team members at Online for Life have abortion in their pasts. Despite the pain they often feel when sharing their stories, they do so willingly, knowing that their story may save another person's life. They share with compassion and grace, knowing their testimony might disturb others or even offend some people. They understand, however, that innocently causing offense is far more acceptable than saying nothing and allowing a child to perish in the womb.

Churches concerned about offending their flock by teaching about abortion should consider delivering the message laced with forgiveness and grace. Abortion is a deadly sin. But it is not beyond Jesus Christ's forgiveness. There are millions of people sitting in pews across America who are suffering in silence from abortion. If pastors and priests start the conversation by sharing forgiveness, healing, and restoration from abortion through Christ, their faith communities will be far more apt to talk candidly about the sacredness of human life and what the church can do to protect unborn children.

The gospel is inherently offensive. Calling fellow sinners to repentance, preaching the Good News, and being engaged in any gospel work can and does cause offense. Preaching and teaching about abortion my offend some. Though our words and actions must be laced with grace and compassion, we still must accept that the life of the Christian includes conflict.

3. To teach about abortion is self-indicting.

With over fifty-six million aborted babies in America over the past four decades, it is likely there is a large number of pastors, elders, deacons, and other church leaders with abortions in their pasts.

Maybe they have repressed the pain of their abortion decision. Maybe they are pro-abortion because they don't want to acknowledge their own guilt. Perhaps they have sought forgiveness but are still ashamed to talk about it. Whatever the reason, they will not discuss it in public. To do so brings back very difficult memories and is a source of embarrassment and shame to some.

4. "Abortion is not a core issue for us."

That statement is impossible to reconcile in light of the millions of children who have lost their lives to abortion, but it is a very common position in faith communities. The church may focus on foreign or local missions, feeding the poor, evangelism, or working with single women. And these are all very good, biblical things that need the church's attention.

As I've said numerous times in public, however, abortion is not "an issue." It is *the* issue. Abortion in America has claimed nine times the number of lives lost in the Jewish Holocaust. We abort more children every day than all the victims who perished on 9/11. Abortion's links to drug and alcohol abuse, depression, suicide, divorce, emotional and physical maladies, and relational destruction are incontrovertible. I documented these links in great detail in *Abortion: The Ultimate Exploitation of Women*, and I invite you to review that book for a complete picture of the insidious personal destruction caused by abortion. There isn't a person alive in America today who hasn't been touched by abortion, either through direct loss or the absence of someone who should be alive today. How many best friends, roommates, spouses, missionaries, doctors, firemen, nurses, and teachers have we lost to death in the womb?

If a church truly cares about its community, family, and neighborhood, it must lead the effort to end abortion in its city.

5. We focus on the reductionist Gospel.

I've covered this in detail already, but it is worth repeating. To preach the good news of Jesus Christ and His salvation but not preach and teach the priceless value of each and every human being is an incomplete gospel. The gospel of the kingdom is centered on the life, death, and resurrection of Jesus Christ, and that includes Christ's ongoing, powerful redemption and reconciliation of all things. Rescuing families from abortion through education, tangible help, compassion, and even protest are kingdom-building activities.

A church that focuses on preaching the plan of salvation but ignores the perils of abortion does grievance to our Savior and Lord.

6. "If she accepts Jesus, she won't abort."

Remember that conversation my father had with the young theology student at the seminary class? When my father pressed him on why the church shouldn't preach and teach about abortion, the young man answered back, "Well, we share the gospel with her. She will accept Jesus and then keep her child." In my experience, this is a very prevalent theme among evangelicals. If we share Jesus with a woman in crisis, she will accept Him as Savior. And then she will change her mind and not abort her child.

While that is sometimes true, it is an extremely dangerous, simplistic assumption.

Consider these questions: If everyone who accepts Jesus affirms life, why is abortion rampant in the church? Did you struggle with lying, cheating, stealing, or gossiping before you became a Christian? Did you still struggle with any of those things after you accepted Christ?

Do we not still sin after our conversion? Of course we do. Christ sometimes delivers us from struggles with various temptations.

Sometimes He doesn't. And despite our new life in Christ, we continue to be at war with our sinful nature. We continue to sin and will continue to do so until we take our last earthly breath.

Plenty of Christians abort their children. Plenty of abortion-minded women accept Christ and walk right back into a coercive situation with family members who are pressuring them to abort.

Make no mistake—accepting Christ does not guarantee a stay of execution for the child. This is why discipleship and compassionate intervention on behalf of the church is so necessary. This is precisely why the gospel must be preached and taught in its fullness. Christ is not just Savior. He is Lord of all. And He has commissioned His church to be His redeeming people in a lost world.

We aren't called to make converts. We are called to make disciples.

7. We aren't sure what to do.

This is a legitimate concern for many churches that desperately want to see abortion ended in their city and Christ glorified but aren't sure how to get started. On a macro-cultural level, almost any church can develop a strategic plan to influence their local community for life.

Engage the Seven Mountains

It is a terrible travesty that many churches have receded from the cultural, social, and political realms. The church is the voice of the Bible, morality, compassion, truth, and grace, and its silence on moral concerns has created predictable results: sexual excess, greed, immorality, and a culture of death.

This unbiblical segmentation of American life can be undone. Churches can once again take the lead in being the voice of the Bible in all spheres of influence.

In the mid-1970s, Bill Bright, Loren Cunningham, and Francis Schaeffer developed a strategy that is now known by several different names, but let's stick with the "Seven Mountain Strategy." The Seven Mountains are areas of life that have the greatest influence on a nation. Bright, Cunningham, and Schaeffer concluded that if the church was to truly have a monumental, positive impact on a nation, the church was to be influential in all seven mountains. These mountains (or spheres of influence) are: Church, Business, Education, Government, Arts and Entertainment, Family, and Media. A local church can, if it so chooses, have an enormous impact on all seven mountains.

Seen through the lens of abortion, we must ask ourselves whether or not the church or the culture has had the greatest influence in these seven areas.

1. Church:

The majority of Protestant churches have non-biblical or nonexistent doctrinal statements regarding the sacredness of human life. Most denominations have no national, concerted effort to be a voice for the unborn.

2. Business:

The overwhelming majority of local and national companies do not take a position on the abortion holocaust because of its supposed political overtones.

3. Education:

Our education system is run by the federal government. That government legalized abortion on demand and continues to push an evolutionist, humanist view of mankind. They indoctrinate our children with the message that life is without eternal consequence and that we can value life as we see fit.

4. Government:

Substantial progress is being made to protect the unborn at the state level. The life-affirming community has made great gains within various states, though there has been virtually no progress at the federal level.

5. Arts and Entertainment:

The Christian and life-affirming community have made great strides in this area of influence. Major movies such as *Bella* and *October Baby* have received critical acclaim as well as broad releases. Television shows such as *Duck Dynasty* deliver family-oriented, life-affirming messages to the masses. Though Hollywood and the mainstream media continue to drive the abortion agenda, that message is losing steam in light of well-produced, positive media productions.

Multi-Grammy-award-winning artist and former lead singer of Kansas, John Elefante, recently released a song called "This Time" and produced a video about his adopted daughter, Sami. Sami was the child of a teenage mom who almost aborted her. Though Christian music networks refused to play the song because it was too "controversial," Online for Life teamed up with John to get the song out to the masses. The video has been viewed on YouTube almost 500,000 times and continues to make an impact worldwide.

6. Family:

As the man goes, so goes the family. While America enjoys millions of men who are committed to their God, their wives, and their families, we are also still plagued by a culture that feminizes, demeans, and emasculates men. We need only remind ourselves that 85 percent of abortions are performed on single women. We have a massive father problem in the United States.

7. Media:

In my book *Media Revolution: A Battle Plan to Defeat Mass Deception in America*, I wrote about the "democratization of media." The mainstream TV, radio, print, and Internet media channels in our country continue to disperse among the masses. Whereas just a few TV networks controlled the entire message and news cycle just thirty years ago, today everyone contributes to and broadcasts the news. This massive and continual dispersion of media control presents an enormous opportunity for life-affirming churches. Though the mainstream channels continue to strongly espouse a pro-abortion position, it is now possible to reach virtually every person in America through alternative media channels.

So how can a church engage in the seven mountains? By prayerfully determining how a particular church is gifted and applying those gifts to one or more mountains. Lead the effort to develop a seven-mountain plan in your church. Gather your leaders and determine how God is calling your parish to be a life-affirming influence outside the walls of your church. Most likely you have all of the talents and skills you need already sitting in your pews.

Perhaps your church is politically motivated. Help to get a member elected to the local school board. Assist local life-affirming politicians in their campaigns. Recruit a group of members to attend the annual March for Life in Washington, DC. Have a church committee vet local, state, and federal judges to see whether or not they are ruling biblically and affirming life. Do the same for local, state, and federal lawmakers. Organizations such as Family Research Council (www.frc.org) can assist with that work.

Maybe your church has a heart for the family. Contact the Fatherhood Initiative (www.Fatherhood.org), Focus on the Family (www.fotf.org), Family Talk (www.DrJamesDobson.org) or a host of other local and national organizations dedicated to ending the fatherhood crisis in America. They will have a stable full of ideas that your church can implement in your area.

Business: You have numerous business owners in your churches and parishes. Those businesses have young women in them who are, at this moment, contemplating abortion. Those businesses also employ mothers and fathers of aborted babies. Those businesses can be a resource for moms in crisis and a place of healing for post-abortive parents. Insecurity drives a woman's abortion decision, and insecurity is caused by any number of pressures, including financial, relational, parental, or social. Your business could partner with your local pro-life pregnancy resource center to provide the location, materials, food, and babysitting for a financial training class, relational counseling, or baby showers for moms. Moms in crisis need a support network, and you can help them connect to one. Consider working with your local youth groups to sponsor fun, educational events about pregnancy, parenting, abstinence, and sexual health, and help prevent unplanned pregnancy.

Provide confidential, free counseling to your employees; many of them are post-abortive. By letting your employees know you are making this service available, you may well be the conduit for their healing. Many post-abortive parents don't realize that abortion is a root cause of their challenges, and biblically-based, competent counseling can help unveil their hurt and pain so that peace can be restored to your employees' hearts and minds.

Business owners, your business is not separate from your church. There is no division between secular and sacred (Ps. 24:1). God has given you your company, and it is an extension of the church. Your business is a conduit to rescue unborn babies from being killed in the womb, and it is also a place of healing and comfort.

For a church working on a local, community level, allow me to present this battle plan: Seven Steps to Ending Abortion. These seven actions are: Learn, Pray, Heal, Rescue, Teach, Give, and Disciple.

Step 1: Learn

As we've noted, ignorance about abortion, its impact on women and the family, and its destructive power is harmful and deadly. If the church is to grow in its influence and impact to protect families, we must educate ourselves, our small groups, our congregations, and our church leadership about the silent holocaust.

One simple way to start the learning process is to make sure your church or denomination has developed and teaches a doctrinal statement related to the sacredness of human life. It may seem rather bland to suggest that the first step in a church's movement into the abortion-ending arena is to document its biblical position regarding abortion. But we act according to our beliefs, and beliefs are hard to quantify if they aren't written down.

This step is largely for Protestant churches, as the Catholic Church's position is codified in Rome. Most every Protestant church has a doctrinal statement on core tenets of the Christian faith. This is often crafted and refined at the denomination's central offices, but there are hundreds of nondenominational or unaffiliated churches that draft their own statements.

If your denomination or church does not have a clear, concise, completely life-affirming statement regarding the sacredness of human life and abortion, be the change agent in your church. Lead the charge to develop and implement it. If you want some existing statements to start with, check the life-affirming denominations I've included in this book. The Southern Baptist statement is particularly clear and cogent, though most of the pro-life denominations or groups have solid statements.

A few pointers:

- A life-affirming Christian believes that all human life is sacred, regardless of the circumstance of the conception or the health condition of the child. That means that children conceived from rape, incest, or other travesties have inherent dignity and deserve the church's love, protection, and compassion. God, in His mysterious and divine plan, uses the worst of humanity to bring about redemption, new life, and blessing. That is an amazingly wonderful aspect of God—He brings beauty from ashes.

  Children with Down syndrome, genetic abnormalities, terminal illness, or other health conditions have the same priceless value as children without those conditions. They are to be given the same right to life as every other child. This in no way minimizes the difficulty and challenge that hand-icapped children may inherently bring to a family. Yet it also provides an opportunity for a church to show the tangible, committed work of Christ to that family and, in so doing, glorify our Maker.

- As I'll note below, the church should not ignore those families suffering from a past abortion. A statement regarding abortion may contain an assurance that there is redemption, healing, and forgiveness through Jesus Christ for those family members who participated in abortion.

There are any number of other ways to get educated about the abortion epidemic in America and around the world. I've included a list of excellent books in the Resources section at the end of this book.

Numerous pro-life groups have an abundance of resources on their websites and send out regular email updates. I am constantly on www.LifeSiteNews.com for current information, stories, and perspectives. Though Dr. Jim Denison comments on numerous cultural and social issues, he frequently discusses abortion and life-related issues. Sign up for his free newsletter at www.DenisonForum.org. Online for Life and our church outreach, Multiply Life, provide regular updates and commentary as well (www.OnlineForLife.org and www.MultiplyLife.com). A list of other recommended sites are included in the Resources section.

One of the best ways to learn about how abortion impacts your community is to contact your local pro-life pregnancy center. Schedule a visit with the executive director and ask him or her to tell you about their work, their perspective on abortion in your area, and how they see abortion impacting women and men. Their insights will be invaluable.

There is no shortage of resources, tools, and information about abortion in today's tech-savvy environment. Take advantage of these powerful information sources and become articulate about abortion's spiritually, emotionally, and physically destructive impact on us all. If you are like me, your heart will melt and you will want to take the next step.

Step 2: Pray

We cannot possibly underestimate the power of prayer, especially when it comes to abortion and families in crisis.

Your church can rescue families from abortion through prayer. I've seen it happen. Countless volunteers and staff members at life-affirming pregnancy centers can testify to the power of prayer.

God hears and answers prayers. And churches across America can make a game-changing, life-altering difference in the abortion epidemic by committing their hearts and minds to prayer.

Here are a few suggestions to help you and your church become prayer warriors:

- Each morning, say a short prayer with your family for any families in your area that are considering abortion. Pray that they will choose life and that those families will be provided with the tangible help they need.

- Connect with your local pregnancy center and ask that they send you prayer requests each week. Pray for those needs with your Sunday school, small group, women's ministry, men's ministry, or family. Ask if those needs can be printed in a church bulletin or on a church website, so that the entire church family can be praying for families in crisis.

- Organize or join a 40 Days for Life group (www.40DaysForLife. com) in your area. This rapidly growing, well-trained prayer movement is saving babies in cities across America in large numbers. Joining or forming a group will also help connect you to other churches in your area and begin to build a community-driven effort outside of just one local church.

- Download the free Online for Life prayer app (www.ProLifeApp.com). This revolutionary technology has enabled us to grow a national prayer team of thousands of committed Christians. Online for Life is networked with fifty-plus pregnancy centers and mobile ultrasound units across the country, and we are able to share prayer needs from around the country in real time. Would you like to intercede for a woman in crisis who is, at this moment, contemplating abortion? You can do so with this free app. Plus, you can recruit your praying friends to pray with you, and the app tracks your impact. Want to know how many of the mothers you prayed for chose life for their child? Yeah, we got that.

Step 3: Heal

There are tens of millions of Americans who need Christ's forgiveness for abortion. They need the hope, joy, and peace that only come from Jesus. There is too much hurt, pain, and suffering in our families to avoid talking about abortion in church.

It is unfortunate that many professing "pro-life" Christians refuse to extend grace and mercy to post-abortive people. Online for Life occasionally shares encouragement and grace about those who have chosen abortion on our Facebook page. Though the vast majority of comments are positive and affirming of Christ's love and forgiveness, some are not so charitable:

> "Nobody can make the choice to MURDER your inno-
> cent baby . . . you can get help to leave boyfriends and

husbands and family . . . only you can make that call. Murder is bad no matter how much you pray or ask for forgiveness. They should be made to feel bad and pain from there [*sic*] actions not given a book to make it seem ok to murder a fetus."

"If you regret aborting your baby you shouldn't have done it in the first place"

"Abortion is wrong and I believe you all are going to hell its in our ten comandments though shall not kill [*sic*] you better hope you havent signed up to be satans [*sic*] personal b***"

"All sins are not equal; how dumb! And here is just one of my problems with aborting a healthy, viable pregnancy . . . some women treat killing . . . murdering the most innocent of all innocents, as just another means of birth control. You all know thus [*sic*] to be a fact! Then you have other like-minded individuals sitting around in a support group setting giving each other these positive strokes and doing this feel-good insanity about it not being all that important and that God will give you a pass at the pearly gates as if the murder of the fetus was no more important than a speeding ticket."

We so often want mercy for ourselves but judgment for others. With perspectives and comments like these, is it any wonder why we don't see more post-abortive people seeking help from churches?

Most of us who seek to protect unborn life from death in the womb understand the vehement passion and emotion behind these comments. We want the killing to stop. We want all innocent children to have the opportunity to live and be free from fatal violence. We want parents to do everything humanly possible to protect their children.

Is abortion a sin? Certainly. Should we be committed to rescuing every child within our reach? Yes. Should we offer compelling and convincing evidence to abortion-minded parents so that they choose life? Of course. Do we contemplate with horror the vast numbers of children who have been killed in the name of "choice" and "rights"? We do.

Should we cast vitriol, hate, and judgment at those parents who have aborted a child?

We should not.

As Christians, we acknowledge we are all sinners. We acknowledge we are all lost. We are all dirty, rotten people who are incapable of doing truly honorable good without the presence of Christ. Does this mean that the sin of abortion and the sin of breaking the speed limit are the same? Are we winking at abortion when we extend grace and forgiveness to someone who has aborted, even if that person isn't repentant? I think the reason this is a hard truth for some people is because we think that, by forgiving those who have aborted, we are excusing what they did.

Our review of Scripture clearly shows that God takes killing very seriously. Capital punishment was instituted in the Old Testament to protect life, and punishments for less grievous sins were far less extreme yet sin is sin. One tiny sin separates us from God and, because of His holiness, places the curse of eternal death on each one of us. That curse is only lifted through the perfect life, death, and resurrection of Jesus Christ.

But all sins are not equal when it comes to earthly punishment and discipline. I won't get life in prison if I steal gum from a convenience store, and I won't get a twenty-five-dollar fine if I kill someone with my car. God's law for mankind provides greater punishment for more severe crimes. Modern Western law is based on the same concept. In that sense, abortion is among the severest of sins by Scripture's standards. Destroying God's beautiful, crowning creation in her smallest, weakest state is an offense to a holy God.

But abortion is not beyond the power of the cross. Though we all deserve hell because of just one sin, a person who aborts a child is no more deserving of hell than a person who hasn't. Christ came to save sinners, and that includes post-abortive parents. As much as we hate and detest abortion, we do not hate and detest those who have aborted.

Even if United States law allows us to escape any consequence for abortion, do not fool yourself. Abortion brings pain, suffering, and consequences of its own, even if the law does not. As horrible and tragic as abortion is, as complicit and guilty as parents who abort their children are, and as death-loving as we've become as a society, we must maintain a delicate but necessary balance.

We must be relentless in our pursuit to end abortion. We must also be relentless in our pursuit to show love, grace, and forgiveness to those who, at some point, chose abortion. And that relentless pursuit must start in pulpits, Sunday school classes, and small groups through the church. Millions of people sitting in pews or in homes need to hear about the healing, redemption, and peace found in Jesus Christ. They need to be set free from the prison they constructed for themselves. They need to know that abortion is covered under the blood of our Savior.

Start a post-abortive recovery group for women and men. Post-abortive women and men may suffer in many ways, including alcoholism, drug abuse, depression, relationship challenges, anger, bitterness, or an inappropriate work ethic. By offering hope and healing, your church has the opportunity to extend tremendous freedom to parents and family members who are prisoners to abortion. The need for churches to be places of help, healing, and restoration is enormous. What a wonderful opportunity for churches to share the forgiveness of Christ to hurting people!

I've included a partial list of post-abortive recovery sites, curricula, and resources in the back of this book. Please take a moment to look them over and order a few. See which may be appropriate resources for your church.

If your church hasn't provided a post-abortive healing class before, it may take some courage to start one. Most post-abortive parents do not want anyone to know about their past. You may find one-on-one opportunities more helpful at first. As a church becomes known for its effective post-abortive ministry, however, people are more inclined to come out of the woodwork and come to group classes.

This is also a fabulous opportunity to reach the unchurched in your area. If you choose to start a post-abortive healing class, consider doing some simple, discreet outreach into your neighborhoods. Ads can be placed online, in local newspapers, or in other channels. A sample ad might say:

> Struggling with a past abortion? We can help.
> Confidential, nonjudgmental, compassionate.
> Email or call.
> You can experience freedom from your pain.

Women and men who have experienced abortion are often scared to darken the doors of a church for fear of judgment or retribution. Be the hands and feet of Christ by providing them a safe place to come and experience the presence of Christ.

Step 4: Rescue

The body of Christ can participate directly in the rescuing of children and families from abortion.

First, the church should create an environment where parents, both inside and outside the church, know the church wants to work with and care for women and men facing unplanned pregnancies. Many, many women in crisis pregnancies assume they will be put to shame if they step into a church. Therefore church leadership should consistently let their congregations know that women in crisis will be welcomed with open arms.

Families should be encouraged to speak to their children (at the appropriate age) about sexual purity, marriage, and unplanned pregnancies. Youth groups, small groups, and college-aged ministries should regularly address sexuality and pregnancy. Though the church should teach sexual purity, it must also strongly encourage a compassionate attitude towards those who are unexpectedly pregnant.

Second, think about starting a specific ministry for families in crisis. One example of a church-based ministry that supports, trains, and provides substantial support for women in unexpected pregnancy situations is based in Southlake, TX. Embrace Grace (www.IEmbraceGrace. com) may be one of the most relevant and tangible expressions of the gospel I've seen in the life-affirming world. Amy Ford, the founder and president of Embrace Grace, got pregnant and made the decision to abort. Her miraculous experience in the abortion clinic (resulting in her choosing life) led her to find a way to connect the church with women in crisis pregnancy situations. Embrace Grace is led by women who have all "been there," and they lavish care, compassion, and love on young women in difficult circumstances. While Embrace Grace provides biblical education to women who generally have none, they provide much more, including a safe place where women can plug into a support network of friends. Embrace Grace works with and inside the local church, so women in crisis experience transformation and hope within its walls.

Third, consider partnering with your local pro-life pregnancy center. If your church does not have the staff and resources to counsel women and men in crisis, the pregnancy center can most likely assist. If you have a good relationship with your local center, help for someone in trouble is a phone call or email away.

Step 5: Teach

As we've already discovered, some Christians have very little sense of the scope and heartbreak caused by abortion. Yet we all have been impacted by it in some shape or form. Our country needs pastors, priests, teachers, leaders, laypeople, and counselors to preach and teach frequently about abortion. Though I'm grateful for Sanctity of Life Sunday in January, 3,500 children lose their lives to abortion every day. Abortion is not a seasonal epidemic to be noted just once a year.

It is a holocaust that requires constant address and reinforcement from the church.

I'm not proposing that it be the only topic covered in a Sunday message. I am saying that churches that are genuinely concerned about their communities make a constant effort to educate their flocks about the silent holocaust.

Here are a few suggestions to get the discussion started:

- Start a semester-long Sunday school class that explores the spiritual ramifications of abortion. Use current facts, stories, and information to support the Bible's clear teachings about the sacredness of all life from conception through natural death.

- Allow and invite people to share their unplanned pregnancy or post-abortive testimonies in appropriate public settings. Numerous babies have been saved from abortion simply because a woman shared a story of how she made it through an unplanned pregnancy, or a man shared about the loss and guilt he felt after losing a child he never had the chance to meet.

- Weave the topic into appropriate sermons, teachings, and messages. Important points about unborn life, the sacredness of human life, and God's passion for life can be shared in the context of hundreds of other topics, including the Incarnation, creation, grace, forgiveness, joy, eternal life, the Crucifixion, family, parenting, marriage, sexual relations, etc.

- Teach abstinence. The overwhelming numbers of abortions occur because of unplanned pregnancy outside of marriage. As our culture becomes increasingly sex-saturated, the church appears to have become untied from its marriage and purity moorings. The fact that abortion has become normalized as sexual purity has eroded is incontrovertible. The more sex occurs outside of marriage, the more children die.

- A word of caution: there is a risk with teaching sexual purity in church if it is not complemented by the assurance of the church's desire to help women in crisis pregnancies. It is a tricky balance. I've spoken with many women who left their churches when they became pregnant out of wedlock because of guilt and shame. While the church must teach sexual purity, the church must also recognize we are all sinners. We must extend compassion, grace, and help to those women who become pregnant, even as we teach purity.

Become old-fashioned. Teach abstinence. Teach sexual purity through marriage. Talk candidly about the spiritual and social destruction of sexual promiscuity, pornography, and illicit affairs.

- Start small groups to explore the sacredness of human life. If your church avoids abortion because it has been politicized, don't start a group about "abortion." Start a group that discusses humans as image-bearers of God. Discuss the priceless value of human life from conception through natural death. I suspect small groups will flourish if the material is presented in tactful, nonpolitical ways. Remember, every person has been touched by abortion in some way at some time. Find creative ways to raise the topic without allowing it to devolve into political arguing.

- Explore ways to talk about abortion through the lens of modern culture. How does abortion impact population control and vice versa? Does abortion elevate or demean women? Is abortion tied to racism? How is abortion tied to pornography? There are myriad ways to explore and discuss abortion in church with intelligence, grace, and winsomeness.

- Embed sacredness-of-life material into existing discipleship and teaching courses. With fifty-six million dead children in the US and hundreds of millions more worldwide, every single basic Bible course, discipleship training, leadership and mentoring course, and Christian education class should include

Biblical information about the sacredness of life, abortion, and the impact of abortion on the church and the world. Because abortion impacts marriage, relationships, spirituality, abuse, social stability, and the fabric of the church, it should be prevalent whenever we train others in the Christian faith.

Step 6: Give

Planned Parenthood, the largest abortion mill in the country, has a $1 billion budget. More than one-third of their budget comes in the form of federal tax dollars. The leading pro-abortion research firm, the Guttmacher Institute, has an annual budget of around $14 million. Most pro-life pregnancy centers have budgets under $100,000. As best as I've been able to determine, the largest national pro-life organization has a budget of around $10 million.

Let that sink in. The abortion industry's *research group* has a larger budget than the nation's largest pro-life organization.

That isn't to say people don't give to pro-life groups, because there are thousands of them scattered across the country. However, many, if not most, of these groups are underfunded, considering the weight and scope of their missions. Because most pro-life denominations do not have a coordinated pro-life stewardship program nationally, giving is determined at the local level by the local church. This means the giving commitment to various pro-life efforts can differ widely based on the church and location. Individuals and families normally account for many pro-life groups' donations. At Online for Life, the number of churches who give to our work is less than 0.5 percent of the entire group of donors.

I suspect most churches do not allocate a large portion of a missions, outreach, or community budget to pro-life work. I'm not making a judgment on a church's stewardship policy, but I would advise church leadership to evaluate their budgets in light of the abortion epidemic. The fact is that ending abortion requires substantial prayer and funds. And life-affirming work is a wonderful manifestation of the gospel.

Life-affirming organizations normally fall into one of three categories: community, activist, and political. We need all three working cooperatively together in order to accomplish our mission.

Community groups include pro-life pregnancy centers, in-church ministries like Embrace Grace, and national organizations that support and serve local communities such as Online for Life. These groups work directly with women and men in crisis situations, extending compassion, grace, and tangible help to the public.

Activist groups work to educate the public about the dangers and horrors of abortion, the lies of the abortion industry, abuses at abortion clinics, and the benefits of a life-affirming culture. Bloggers such as Jill Stanek and organizations like Live Action are examples of activists. They are a very necessary part of the movement, as they are sources of vital information and perspective.

Political groups work to influence legislation and political races on behalf of the unborn. Groups such as Americans United for Life or the Law of Life Project may focus on legal cases or federal and state bills. Groups like the National Right to Life also work to influence local, state, and federal elections.

Strong and sacrificial financial support is necessary to fuel this holistic effort and combat the federal government-backed abortion mill, Planned Parenthood.

Giving your vote is also an essential aspect of the pro-life Christian. I am always stunned at the enormous number of Christians who don't vote and distressed at the number of Christians who vote for pro-abortion candidates. Christians must vote, and vote pro-life. If you accept the biblical fact that Jesus is Lord of all, then you accept that Jesus is Lord of the political sphere and government. And if He has called His church to be salt and light in the world, then we have an obligation to influence our government for Christ, and our primary vehicle for doing so is through our votes.

If you don't vote because you believe in the separation of church and state, see my earlier comments on this topic. Our founding fathers fully intended the church to be a strong voice and influence on government—in fact they relied on it. The phrase "separation of church and state" does not appear in any founding document, and its modern interpretation is simply a tool by humanists to drive their secular agenda. Remember, for the Christian there is no sacred and secular. There is only sacred. God is in charge of our government, and He has commissioned you and me to be stewards over it. Get out and vote.

To vote for a particulate candidate is to approve and validate his or her positions and platforms. If you vote for a pro-abortion candidate, you cast your vote for abortion. You are, by virtue of our representative government, putting someone in office who supports the killing of God's image-bearers.

Many Christians argue that we can't be one-issue voters. When choosing a candidate for office, we must consider the candidate's perspectives on the role of government, the economy, the environment, second amendment rights, and a host of other very important issues. Certainly we need to understand a prospective candidate's positions on all essential issues. We need to make informed choices when we vote.

However, as I've maintained throughout this book, abortion is the primary spiritual, cultural, and familial issue of our age. And the right to life, as articulated in the Declaration of Independence, is the first of all of the inalienable rights. In other words, if your favorite political candidate is in favor of fatally discriminating against the weakest among us, he or she is rejecting the foundational right upon which all other rights are based. And to vote for a pro-abortion candidate is, quite simply, to reject the clear teachings of the Bible. Your pro-abortion vote leads to the death of millions.

Vote every election. And vote only for pro-life candidates.

Step 7: Disciple

Almost every major city in the United States has at least one pro-life pregnancy center. These local clinics seek to reach out to women and men in crisis, provide them counsel and support, and rescue children who are at risk to be aborted. Many pregnancy centers do not have the budgets or staff to be able to commit to walking alongside an at-risk family through or after a crisis. Yet local pregnancy centers tend to be the best place to get connected to such a family. Consider reaching out to your local life-affirming center and asking how you can become involved. Ask them how you can directly help a single mother or a struggling father as they consider whether or not to choose life for their child.

Men, we probably are all well-acquainted with the problem of lost fatherhood in America. Millions of women are getting pregnant by men who neglect or ignore their role and responsibility. Your willingness to come alongside a young man or a young couple can be the difference between life and death. Men, you may be the first male a young woman or man has met who exemplifies what a real husband and father should be. Your time, encouragement, example, and compassion may just save a child from death and a family from heartache.

One by One (www.OneByOneUSA.org) works with churches to develop and recruit mentors to work with families that come through life-affirming pregnancy centers. They have developed curricula for coaching women and couples facing unplanned pregnancies and the challenges of life with newborns. They have effectively connected churches to at-risk families while providing substantial support through education materials and the church itself. Their passion and commitment to both the church and the pregnancy center is inspirational and effective.

Your city or town may already have a ministry that connects Christian men and women with families in crisis. If not, consider contacting Embrace Grace or One by One, or working with your church to adapt some other existing program for your community. Or you can just walk into your local pregnancy center and tell them you are ready to link arms with someone who needs a friend!

Of course, discipleship is not limited to families in crisis. As part of developing followers of Christ, teachings about the sacredness of human life and the evil of abortion must be included in even the most basic discipleship curricula. If your church has a catechism, small group training, men's and women's discipleship courses, basis of the Christian faith material, or topical studies on marriage, family, sexuality, or parenting, each one should include strong, biblical teaching on the sacredness of life and the basics about abortion. If any such course fails to address the leading cause of death in America, consider supplementing it with your own material approved by church leadership. Online for Life continues to develop materials that can be used in church, so keep checking www.MultiplyLife.com.

∼

Some think the answer to ending abortion is to overturn *Roe v. Wade*, defund Planned Parenthood, win abortion debates, or shut down local abortion clinics. Those are all very worthy and appropriate goals, and I would love to see each one happen in the next few years.

Yet those goals will not be accomplished without the church. Abortion will not be ended without the church. Babies will continue to perish, parents will continue to suffer, and the moral fabric of our nation will continue to decay unless the church takes the compassionate lead to defend the unborn and their families.

If abortion is primarily a spiritual concern, then the church is primarily responsible for addressing it. The church, commissioned by Christ to be His hands and feet, is the frontline means by which the grace, compassion, tangible help, truth, and protection of the gospel permeate our culture.

I'm frequently asked if abortion really can be ended in America. My answer is always this statement: "Of course, yes."

The follow-up question is almost always the same. "How?"

The answer is simple. "When the church of Jesus Christ refuses to remain silent any longer and commits to following His commands."

May we as Christians follow His commands. Millions of lives depend on us.

Resources

This list is by no means exhaustive or authoritative. Rather these are books, sites, and resources that our staff at Online for Life has read, reviewed, or uses on a regular basis. Consider this a starter list, and I invite you to seek out other works, organizations, and websites to continue your education.

Abortion Recovery Resources

Her Choice to Heal: Finding Spiritual and Emotional Peace after Abortion
Synda Massa & Joan Phillips

Forgiven and Set Free
Linda Cochrane

Surrendering the Secret
Pat Layton

Worthy of Love: Finding Hope after Abortion
Shadia Hrichi

You're Not Alone: Healing through God's Grace After Abortion
Jennifer O'Neill

Breaking Free
Beth Moore

Ramah International
www.RamahInternational.org

Rachel's Vineyard
www.RachelsVineyard.org

Project Rachel
National Office of Post-Abortion Reconciliation and Healing
www.noparh.org

Abortion Memorial
www.AbortionMemorial.com

Abortion Changes You
www.AbortionChangesYou.com

Pro-Life Books That Cover the Basics
The Case for Life
Scott Klusendorf

Abortion: The Ultimate Exploitation of Women
Brian Fisher

Pro Life Answers to Pro Choice Arguments
Randy Alcorn

Abortion: A Rational Look at an Emotional Issue
R. C. Sproul and Greg Bailey

Innocent Blood
John Ensor

Unplanned
Abby Johnson

Major Pro-Life News Sites
LifeSiteNews
www.LifeSiteNews.com

Live Action News
www.LiveActionNews.org

LifeNews.com
www.LifeNews.com

National Right to Life
www.nrlc.org

Abort73
www.Abort73.com

Endnotes

1. Bernard Nathanson, MD, with Richard Ostling, *Aborting America* (New York: Doubleday, 1979), 161.
2. Ibid.
3. Bernard Nathanson, "Pro-Choice 1990," *New Dimensions* (October 1990): 38. Cited in John Ensor, *Innocent Blood* (Cruciform, 2011), 93. Kindle Edition.
4. R.C. Sproul, Jr. "Who Will Stand," short video on sidewalk counselor John Barros. https://www.youtube.com/watch?v=L37FfyAbZvc.
5. Quotes From Church Documents About Issues Of Human Life, Justice And Peace, United States Conference of Catholic Bishops, http://www.usccb.org/beliefs-and-teachings/what-we-believe/quotes-issues-human-life-justice-and-peace.cfm.
6. "Roe v. Wade at 40: Most Oppose Overturning Abortion Decision," Pew Forum Religion and Public Life Project, January 16, 2013, http://www.pewforum.org/2013/01/16/roe-v-wade-at-40/#age.
7. "Prenatal Form and Function—The Making of an Earth Suit," Endowment for Human Development, http://www.ehd.org/dev_article_intro.php.
8. "Prenatal Summary," Endowment for Human Development, http://www.ehd.org/prenatal-summary.php. Note that fetal ages have been adjusted to reflect time from fertilization rather than gestational age, which is measured from the start of the last normal menstrual period.
9. "Abortion Surveillance—United States, 2009," Centers for Disease Control and Prevention, http://www.cdc.gov/mmwr/preview/mmwrhtml/ss6108a1.htm. Gestational age is measured from the start of the last normal menstrual period. It is generally two weeks greater than the age from conception since fertilization typically takes place fourteen days after the prior menstruation.
10. "America Won't Reject Abortion Until It Sees Abortion," Fr. Frank Pavone's Blog, http://www.priestsforlife.org/blog/index.php/america-wont-reject-abortion-until-it-sees-abortion.
11. "In-Clinic Abortion Procedures," Planned Parenthood Federation of America, http://www.plannedparenthood.org/health-topics/abortion/in-clinic-abortion-procedures-4359.asp.
12. C. Everett Koop, MD, and Francis A. Schaeffer, *Whatever Happened to the Human Race?* (Westchester, IL: Crossway Books, 1979, 1983), 18.
13. "Abortion Surveillance—United States, 2009," Centers for Disease Control and Prevention. http://www.cdc.gov/mmwr/preview/mmwrhtml/ss6108a1.htm.
14. Rachel K. Jones and Kathryn Kooistra, "Abortion Incidence and Access to Services In the United States, 2008," *Perspectives on Sexual and Reproductive Health* 43, no. 1 (March 2011): 48, http://www.guttmacher.org/pubs/journals/4304111.pdf.

15. "In-Clinic Abortion Procedures," PlannedParenthood.org.

16. Jones and Kooistra, "Abortion Incidence," 48, http://www.guttmacher.org/pubs/journals/4304111.pdf.

17. Tony Levatino, "A Medical Doctor describes the Dilation and Evacuation Procedure," PriestsforLife.org, http://www.priestsforlife.org/resources/medical/delevatino.htm.

18. Warren M. Hern, MD, and Billie Corrigan, RN, MS, "What about us? Staff reactions to D & E," *Advances in Planned Parenthood* XV, no. 1 (1980): 7.

19. Cheryl Sullenger, "Gosnell Worker: Baby Surviving Abortion Struggled in Toilet Trying to Live," LifeNews.com, April 19, 2013, http://www.lifenews.com/2013/04/19/gosnell-worker-baby-surviving-abortion-swam-in-toilet-trying-to-live/.

20. "Abortion Surveillance—United States, 2009," Centers for Disease Control and Prevention, http://www.cdc.gov/mmwr/preview/mmwrhtml/ss6108a1.htm.

21. Ibid.

22. "Abortion Procedures," Abort73.com, http://www.abort73.com/abortion/abortion_techniques/.

23. "Europe's Abortion Rules," BBC.com, February 12, 2007, http://news.bbc.co.uk/2/hi/europe/6235557.stm.

24. Doe v. Bolton, 410 US 179, 192 (1973).

25. Cited in Francis J. Beckwith, *Defending Life* (Cambridge UP, 2007): 21.

26. Joseph Dellapenna, *Dispelling the Myths of Abortion History* (Carolina Academic Press, 2006): 746–47. Quoted in "United States Abortion Policy in the International Context," Americans United for Life, August 1, 2012, http://www.aul.org/united-states-abortion-policy-in-the-international-context/.

27. "Poll: Americans Don't Understand Roe," Human Events, April 25, 2006, http://www.humanevents.com/2006/04/25/poll-americans-dont-understand-roe/.

28. Warren Weaver Jr., "High Court Rules Abortions Legal the First 3 Months," *New York Times*, January 23, 1973, http://www.nytimes.com/learning/general/onthisday/big/0122.html#article.

29. NBC News/Wall Street Journal Survey, Study #13018, January 12–15, 2013, http://msnbcmedia.msn.com/i/MSNBC/Sections/A_Politics/_Today_Stories_Teases/Supreme-court-question.pdf.

30. "Abortion," summary of abortion-related polling results at Gallup.com, http://www.gallup.com/poll/1576/abortion.aspx.

31. Alex Jones, *Losing the News: The Future of the News that Feeds Democracy* (New York: Oxford University Press, 2009), 91.

32. Ibid.,92.

33. Reed Irvine and Cliff Kinkaid, "Media Censor One Side in Abortion Debate," Accuracy in Media, October 31, 2000, http://www.aim.org/media-monitor/media-censor-one-side-in-abortion-debate/.

34. Matt Philben and Lauren Enk, "Nets Give Pro-Abortion Wendy Davis 3 Times Coverage of Entire Gosnell Trial," Culture and Media Institute, Media Research Center, July 23, 2012, http://www.mrc.org/articles/nets-give-pro-abortion-wendy-davis-3-times-coverage-entire-gosnell-trial.

35. "A New Ethic for Medicine And Society," *California Medicine* 113, no. 3 (September 1970). Reposted at http://www.ewtn.com/library/PROLIFE/ NEWETHIC.TXT.

36. Cynthia Gorney, *Articles of Faith: A Frontline History of the Abortion Wars* (New York: Simon and Schuster, 2000), 401.

37. "Abortion" National Abortion Federation, http://www.prochoice.org/Pregnant/ options/abortion.html.

38. "Abortion," Planned Parenthood, http://www.plannedparenthood.org/health- topics/abortion-4260.asp.

39. K. Kaufmann, *The Abortion Resource Handbook* (Touchstone, 1970), 37.

40. "Abortion for Profit," Abort73, September 3, 2010, http://www.abort73.com/ abortion/abortion_for_profit/.

41. Mark Crutcher, "Baby Body Parts for Sale," LifeDynamics.com, February 2000, updated March 2007, http://www.lifedynamics.com/abortion_information/ baby_body_parts/.

42. "New York City Abortion Ratio Declined Slightly In 2011," NYC41Percent. com, March 7, 2013, http://www.nyc41percent.com/.

43. Lawrence B. Finer et al., "Reasons U.S. women have abortions: quantitative and qualitative perspectives," *Perspectives on Sexual and Reproductive Health* 37, no. 3 (September 2005): 110–18. Cited in "Facts on Induced Abortion in the United States August 2011," Guttmacher Institute, http:// www. guttmacher.org/.

44. *Planned Parenthood of Southeastern Pa. v. Casey*, 505 U.S. 833 (1992). FindLaw.com. http://caselaw.lp.findlaw.com/scripts/getcase.pl?court=US&vol =505&invol–833.

45. Sarah Terzo, "Most Women Get Late-Term Abortions for Birth Control Reasons," LifeNews.com, July 15, 2013, http://www.lifenews.com/2013/07/15/ most-women-get-late-term-abortions-for-birth-control-reasons/.

46. James Agresti, "Most Late-Term Abortions Are Not Done for Medical Reasons," LifeNews.com, August 10, 2012, http://www.lifenews.com/2012/08/10/most- late-term-abortions-are-not-done-for-medical-reasons/.

47. Rayna Rapp, *Testing Women, Testing the Fetus: The Social Impact of Amniocentesis in America* (New York: Routledge, 2000), 226.

48. R. Seth Williams, "Report of the Grand Jury," In the Court of Common Pleas, First Judicial District of Pennsylvania, Criminal Trial Division, In Re: Misc. No. 0009901-2008, Grand Jury xxiii : C17, http://www.phila.gov/ districtattorney/PDFs/GrandJuryWomensMedical.pdf.

49. Ibid.

50. Tracy Connor, "Abortion doctor Kermit Gosnell convicted of first-degree murder," NBCNews.com, May 13, 2013, http://usnews.nbcnews.com/_ news/2013/05/13/18232657-abortion-doctor-kermit-gosnell-convicted-of- first-degree-murder?lite.

51. Sarah Hoye, "Philadelphia doctor performed illegal late-term abortions, ex-employee testifies," CNN.com, April 19, 2013, http://www.cnn. com/2013/04/18/us/pennsylvania-abortion-doctor.

52. "Defending Life 2014," Americans United for Life, 6, http://aul.org/defendinglife.

53. Wendy Saltzman, "Delaware abortion clinic facing charges of unsafe and unsanitary conditions," 6ABC.com, WPVI-TV, July 24, 2013, http://abclocal.go.com/wpvi/story?section=news/local&id=9059172.

54. John S. Hausman, "Muskegon official: Abortion clinic was 'a filthy mess,' won't reopen," MLive.com, January 3, 2013, http://www.mlive.com/news/muskegon/index.ssf/2013/01/muskegon_official_abortion_cli.html.

55. John S. Hausman, "Documents, photos detail Muskegon abortion clinic's allegedly unsanitary conditions," MLive.com, January 7, 2013, http://www.mlive.com/news/muskegon/index.ssf/2013/01/muskegon_city_documents_detail.html.

56. Steve Ertelt, "Abortion 'Doctor' Leaves Decapitated Unborn Baby Inside Mother," LifeNews.com, May 2, 2013, http://www.lifenews.com/2013/05/02/abortion-doctor-leaves-decapitated-unborn-baby-inside-mother/.

57. "Another Gosnell: Report Shows Texas Abortion Doc Kills Babies Born Alive," LifeNews.com, May 15, 2013, http://www.lifenews.com/2013/05/15/another-gosnell-report-shows-texas-abortion-doc-kills-babies-born-alive/.

58. Ibid.

59. Ibid.

60. "Gosnell Not Alone in Late-Term Abortion Brutality," Live Action press release, April 29, 2013, http://www.liveaction.org/press/undercover-investigation-reveals-how-leading-d-c-abortion-doctor-would-leave-babies-born-alive-to-die/.

61. "Inhuman: Undercover in America's Late-Term Abortion Industry—New York," LiveAction Films, April 28, 2013, http://www.youtube.com/watch?v=eipSl72hsmI.

62. John McCormick, "Video: Planned Parenthood Official Argues for Right to Post-Birth Abortion," Weekly Standard, March 29, 2013, http://www.weeklystandard.com/blogs/video-planned-parenthood-official-argues-right-post-birth-abortion_712198.html.

63. "Archbishop Chaput: Babies treated like trash," Vatican Radio, May 6, 2013, http://en.radiovaticana.va/news/2013/05/06/archbishop_chaput:_babies_treated_like_trash/en1-689678 .

64. Alberto Giubilini and Francesca Minerva, "After-birth abortion: why should the baby live?" Journal of Medical Ethics, February 23, 2012, http://jme.bmj.com/content/early/2012/03/01/medethics-2011-100411.full

65. Peter Singer, Practical Ethics (Cambridge, UK: Cambridge UP, 1993), 170–171.

66. Policy Review 32 (Spring 1985): 14–15. Cited in Francis J. Beckwith, Defending Life (New York: Cambridge UP, 2007), 48.

67. Michael Tooley, "Abortion and Infanticide," Philosophy & Public Affairs 2, no. 1 (Autumn 1972), 37.

68. Albert Mohler, "The Age of Infanticide: The Culture of Death Marches On," AlbertMohler.com, February 11, 2004, http://www.albertmohler.com/2004/02/11/the-age-of-infanticide-the-culture-of-death-marches-on/.

69. Jonathan Glover, *Causing Death and Saving Lives* (New York: Penguin, 1977), 158. Cited in Ramesh Ponnuru, *The Party of Death: The Democrats, the Media, the Courts, and the Disregard for Human Life* (Washington, DC: Regnery, 2006), Kindle Location 3994.

70. "History Repeating? The Peculiar Comeback of Eugenics," *New Atlantis* 4 (Winter 2004), 111–12, http://www.thenewatlantis.com/publications/history repeating.

71. Jeff McMahan, *The Ethics of Killing: Problems at the Margins of Life* (New York: Oxford UP, 2002), 342.

72. Jeff McMahan, "Infanticide," *Utilitas* 19, no. 2 (June 2007): 131, http://journals. cambridge.org/action/displayAbstract?fromPage=online&aid=1015116.

73. C. Everett Koop, MD, and Francis A. Schaeffer, *Whatever Happened to the Human Race?* (Westchester, IL: Crossway Books, 1979, 1983), 53.

74. Ibid., 15.

75. "Abortion," summary of abortion-related polling results at Gallup.com, http://www.gallup.com/poll/1576/abortion.aspx#3.

76. Daniel Allott and George Neumayr, "Eugenic Abortion 2.0," *American Spectator*, May 2013, http://spectator.org/archives/2013/05/23/eugenic-abortion-20.

77. Leon Kass, "A More Perfect Human," speech at the US Holocaust Memorial Museum, March 17, 2005. Cited in Ramesh Ponnuru, *The Party of Death: The Democrats, the Media, the Courts, and the Disregard for Human Life* (Washington, DC: Regnery, 2006), Kindle Locations 2298–2300.

78. John Paul II, *The Gospel of Life* (Boston: Pauline Books & Media, 1995), 15.

79. Donald DeMarco and Benjamin Wiker, *Architects of the Culture of Death* (San Francisco: Ignatius, 2004), 18.

80. Charles Colson and Nancy Pearcey, *How Now Shall We Live?* (Wheaton, IL: Tyndale House, 1999), 118.

81. "Abortion and Depression Part 1," Interview With Theresa Burke of Rachel's Vineyard Ministries, *A Zenit Daily Dispatch*, March 4, 2006, http://www. ewtn.com/library/PROLIFE/zabortdepr.htm.

82. Kristan Hawkins, "'BroChoice:' Man Complains Casual Sex More Difficult if Abortions Banned," LifeNews.com, July 11, 2013, http://www.lifenews. com/2013/07/11/brochoice-man-complains-casual-sex-more-difficult-if-abortions-banned/.

83. Rush Limbaugh, "Abortion at the Root of Our Cultural Decay," RushLimbaugh. com, June 14, 2013, http://www.rushlimbaugh.com/daily/2013/06/14/abortion_ at_the_root_of_our_cultural_decay.

84. "Abortion in the United States," Guttmacher Institute, http://www.guttmacher. org/media/presskits/abortion-US/statsandfacts.html.

85. Rodney Stark, *The Rise of Christianity: A Sociologist Reconsiders History* (Princeton, NJ: Princeton UP, 1996), 118.

86. Peter Singer, *Practical Ethics* (Cambridge, UK: Cambridge UP, 1993), 173.

87. "A New Ethic for Medicine and Society," *California Medicine*, September 1970, 67.

88. Ibid., 68.
89. Charles Colson and Nancy Pearcey, *How Now Shall We Live?* (Wheaton, IL: Tyndale House, 1999), 123.
90. https://bound4life.com/statistics/
91. Rachel K. Jones, Lawrence B. Finer, and Susheela Singh, "Characteristics of U.S. Abortion Patients, 2008," Guttmacher Institute, 9–10, http://www.guttmacher.org/pubs/US-Abortion-Patients.pdf.
92. Rachel K. Jones, PhD, and Megan L. Kavanaugh, DrPH, "Changes in Abortion Rates Between 2000 and 2008 and Lifetime Incidence of Abortion," *Obstetrics & Gynecology* 117, no. 6 (June 2011): 1362.
93. Rachel K. Jones, Lawrence B. Finer, and Susheela Singh, "Characteristics of U.S. Abortion Patients, 2008," Guttmacher Institute, 10, http://www.guttmacher.org/pubs/US-Abortion-Patients.pdf.
94. http://www.nae.net/nae-newsletter-archive/spring-2012/1006-behind-closed-doors.
95. "*Roe v. Wade* at 40: Most Oppose Overturning Abortion Decision," Pew Research Religion & Public Life Project, January 16, 2013, http://www.pewforum.org/2013/01/16/roe-v-wade-at-40/.
96. "Public Opinion on Abortion," Pew Research Religion and Public Life Project, July 2013, slide 3. http://features.pewforum.org/abortion-slideshow/slide3.php.
97. "*Roe v. Wade* at 40: Most Oppose Overturning Abortion Decision," Pew Research, January 16, 2013, 3. http://www.pewforum.org/files/2013/01/Roe-v-wade-full.pdf.
98. John Paul II, *Evangelium Vitae*, 4, www.catholicsociety.com.
99. "*Roe v. Wade* at 40: Most Oppose Overturning Abortion Decision," Pew Research Religion & Public Life Project, January 16, 2013, http://www.pewforum.org/2013/01/16/roe-v-wade-at-40/.
100. Gallup Poll of Catholics, 2005. Association of Religion Data Archives, http://www.thearda.com/Archive/Files/Codebooks/GALLUP05_CB.asp.
101. US Congregational Life Survey, conducted by the Research Services office of the Presbyterian Church (USA) in April 2001, http://www.uscongregations.org/pdf/asr-2005-db.pdf.
102. http://onlineforlife.org/podcast/abortion-african-american-community/.
103. Walter Hoye, "Betrayal Trauma," www.issues4life.org/newsletters.html.
104. "sovereign," Merriam-Webster.com, January 3, 2014, http://www.meriamwebster.com.
105. Quoted in the "God's Sovereignty" devotional on the Ligonier Ministries website, http://www.ligonier.org/learn/devotionals/gods-sovereignty/.
106. T. P. Pearce, "Sovereignty of God," in *Holman Illustrated Bible Dictionary*, ed. C. Brand et al. (Nashville, TN: Holman Bible Publishers, 2003).
107. Ibid.
108. "Ps. 24:1," *New American Standard Bible: 1995 update* (LaHabra, CA: Lockman Foundation, 1995).
109. "Ps. 139: 1–18," *New American Standard Bible: 1995 update* (LaHabra, CA: Lockman Foundation, 1995).

110. "Ps. 139: 19–22," *New American Standard Bible: 1995 update* (LaHabra, CA: Lockman Foundation, 1995).

111. "Ps. 139: 13–14," *New American Standard Bible: 1995 update* (LaHabra, CA: Lockman Foundation, 1995).

112. "Job 10:8–12," *New American Standard Bible: 1995 update* (LaHabra, CA: Lockman Foundation, 1995)

113. John Paul II, *Evangelium Vitae*, 1, www.catholicssociety.com.

114. Keith L. Moore and T. V. N. Persaud, *Before We Are Born: Essentials of Embryology and Birth Defects*, 4th ed. (Philadelphia: W.B. Saunders, 1993), 1.

115. William J. Larsen, *Human Embryology*, 2nd ed. (New York: Churchill Livingstone, 1997), 17.

116. Ronan O'Rahilly and Fabiola Müller, *Human Embryology & Teratology*, 2nd ed. (New York: Wiley-Liss, 1996), 8, 29.

117. Bruce M. Carlson, *Patten's Foundations of Embryology*, 6th ed. (New York: McGraw-Hill, 1996), 3.

118. Wayne Grudem, *Politics According to the Bible* (Grand Rapids, MI: Zondervan, 2010), 159.

119. Gleason L. Archer Jr., *New International Encyclopedia of Bible Difficulties* (Grand Rapids, MI: Zondervan, 2011).

120. Wayne Grudem, *Politics According to the Bible* (Grand Rapids, MI: Zondervan, 2010), 160.

121. John Ankerberg and John Weldon, *When Does Life Begin and 39 other tough questions about abortion* (Nashville: Wolgemuth & Hyatt, 1989), 185.

122. C. S. Lewis, *The Magician's Nephew* (New York: HarperCollins, 1955, 1983), 122–123.

123. Steve Corbett & Brian Fikkert, *When Helping Hurts* (Chicago: Moody Publishers, 2009), 33.

124. S. Michael Craven, "Is Jesus a King without a Kingdom?" The Battle for Truth: Overcoming Culturalized Christianity, January 22, 2011, http://www.battlefortruth.org/ArticlesDetail.asp?id=410.

125. Cal Thomas, "What have religious conservatives accomplished?" *Salt Lake City Tribune*, May 4, 2007, http://www.sltrib.com/opinion/ci_5812678.

126. Brian Fisher, "Gospel message will continue," *Tuscaloosa News*, May 11, 2007, http://www.tuscaloosanews.com/article/20070511/NEWS/705110374?p=1&tc=pg#gsc.tab=0.

127. D. James Kennedy, "Equipping the Saints," sermon preached June 20, 2002 and available at djameskennedy.com.

128. D. James Kennedy and Jerry Newcombe, *What If Jesus Had Never Been Born?* (Nashville: Thomas Nelson, 1994), 7.

129. United Methodist Church statement on abortion from *The Book of Discipline of The United Methodist Church*. http://archives.umc.org/interior.asp?mid=1732.

130. Sarah Weddington, *A Question of Choice* (New York: Penguin, 1993), 49.

131. John Jefferson Davis, *Abortion and the Christian* (Phillipsburg, NJ: Presbyterian and Reformed, 1984), 2–3.

132. "Abortion," News Archives, United Methodist Church website, http://archives. umc.org/umns/backgrounders.asp?ptid=2&story={FB3D4877-CA2B-4BBE-B0A6-B74DAB578C6F}&mid=905.

133. "General Synod Statements and Resolutions Regarding Freedom of Choice," United Church of Christ, 2.

134. Leo Rosten, ed., *Religions of America: Ferment and Faith in an Age of Crisis* (New York: Simon & Schuster, 1975), 210.

135. "Presbyterians and Abortion: A Look at Our Church's Past," Presbyterians Pro-Life, http://www.ppl.org/index.php/educational-resources/brochures/83-presbyterians-and-abortion-a-look-at-our-churchs-past.

136. Minutes of the General Assembly of the Presbyterian Church in the United States of America, Vol. 18 (Philadelphia: Presbyterian Board of Publication, 1869), 937.

137. Linda Greenhouse and Reva B. Siegel, *Before Roe v. Wade: Voices that shaped the abortion debate before the Supreme Court's ruling* (Yale Law Library, 2012), 29.

138. Douglas Martin, "Howard Moody, Who Led a Historic Church, Dies at 91," *New York Times*, September 13, 2012, http://www.nytimes.com/2012/09/14/nyregion/howard-moody-minister-of-judson-memorial-church-dead-at-91.html.

139. Walter O. Spitzer and Carlyle L. Saylor, eds. *Birth Control and the Christian* (Wheaton, IL: Tyndale House, 1969), xxv.

140. Ibid., xxviii.

141. Ibid., xxix–xxx.

142. Ibid., xxvi.

143. Ibid., 12.

144. See Bruce K. Waltke, "Reflections From The Old Testament On Abortion," *Journal of the Evangelical Theological Society* 19, no. 1 (Winter 1976), 3–13.

145. John Warwick Montgomery. *Slaughter of the Innocents* (Westchester, IL: Cornerstone Books, 1981), 98.

146. Spitzer and Saylor, eds. *Birth Control and the Christian*, xii.

147. Russell D. Moore, "The Gospel according to Jane Roe: Abortion Rights and the Reshaping of Evangelical Theology," *Southern Baptist Journal of Theology* 7, no. 2 (Summer 2003), 41.

148. Linda Greenhouse and Reva B. Siegel, *Before Roe v. Wade: Voices that shaped the abortion debate before the Supreme Court's ruling* (Yale Law Library, 2012), 73.

149. Ibid., 72.

150. Ibid.

151. Kenneth Woodward, "Sex, Sin, and Salvation," *Newsweek*, November 2, 1998, 37. Cited in Russell D. Moore, "The Gospel according to Jane Roe: Abortion Rights and the Reshaping of Evangelical Theology," *Southern Baptist Journal of Theology* 7, no. 2 (Summer 2003), 42.

152. Norman L. Geisler, *Ethics: Alternatives and Issues* (Grand Rapids, MI: Zondervan, 1971), 218–19.

153. Ibid., 222–23.

154. Cynthia Gorney, *Articles of Faith: A Frontline History of the Abortion Wars* (New York: Simon & Schuster, 1998), 339.

155. Ibid.

156. Harold O. J. Brown, "A Method In Which Killing Represents A Solution: The Soul Of The Unborn And The Soul Of America," *Trinity Journal* 14, no. 2 (Fall 1993).

157. Cynthia Gorney, *Articles of Faith: A Frontline History of the Abortion Wars* (New York: Simon & Schuster, 1998), 341.

158. Francis Schaeffer, *A Christian Manifesto* (Westchester, IL: 1981), 68.

159. Michael J. Gorman and Ann Loar Brooks, *Holy Abortion? A Theological Critique of the Religious Coalition for Reproductive Choice* (Eugene, OR: Wipf and Stock, 2003).

160. Ibid.

161. "doctrine," Merriam-Webster.com, 2014, http://www.merriam-webster.com.

162. Joe Maxwell and Steve Hall,"Still-silent shepherds," *World*, January 25, 2014, http://www.worldmag.com/2014/01/still_silent_shepherds.

163. "Position Statements," Southern Baptist Convention, http://www.sbc.net/aboutus/positionstatements.asp.

164. "Sanctity of Human Life: Abortion and Reproductive Issues," Assembly of God, http://ag.org/top/Beliefs/Position_Papers/pp_downloads/PP_Sanctity_of_Human_Life_Abortion_Reproductive_Issues.pdf.

165. "Abortion Issues," Presbyterian Church (USA), http://www.presbyterian mission.org/ministries/101/abortion-issues/#9.

166. "A social creed for the 21st century," Presbyterian Church (USA), http://www.presbyterianmission.org/ministries/acswp/social creed 21st century/.

167. "Abortion," United Methodist Church website, http://archives.umc.org/interior.asp?mid=1732.

168. Michael J. Gorman and Ann Loar Brooks, *Holy Abortion? A Theological Critique of the Religious Coalition for Reproductive Choice* (Eugene, OR: Wipf and Stock, 2003).

169. "Abortion," The Salvation Army, 2014, http://www1.salvationarmy.org/IHQ/www_ihq_isjc.nsf/vw-sublinks/FE3C992C78838853802577DF0071D796?openDocument.

170. Report of the Ad Interim Committee on Abortion, adopted by the Sixth General Assembly of the Presbyterian Church in America, Grand Rapids, MI, June 19–23, 1978, 11. Available at http://www.prolifeforum.org/churches/statements/pca6thga.asp.

171. "Abortion (1976)," Church of God, http://www.churchofgod.org/index.php/resolution-new/resolution/abortion_1976.

172. "Practical Commitments," Church of God, http://www.churchofgod.org/index.php/site/practical-commitments#sthash.mCZ8gQnb.dpuf.

173. "Abortion," Christian and Missionary Alliance General Council, 1981, http://www.cmalliance.org/about/beliefs/perspectives/abortion.

174. "Abortion: The Challenge and the Response of the Church of the Nazarene," Official Site of the International Church of the Nazarenes, http://nazarene.org/ministries/administration/visitorcenter/questions/abortion/.

175. Ibid.
176. "Views About Abortion by Protestant Denomination," US Religious Landscape Survey: Religious Beliefs and Practices, June 1, 2008. See Appendix 2, Detailed Tables, 146, http://www.pewforum.org/files/2008/06/report2-religious-land scape-appendix.pdf.
177. Joe Maxwell & Steve Hall, "Still-silent shepherds," *World*, posted January 10, 2014, http://www.worldmag.com/2014/01/still_silent_shepherds/page2.

About the Author

An author, speaker, and business leader, Brian Fisher is the co-founder and president of Online for Life.

After graduating college with a degree in music, he quickly discovered that musical talent and musical employment are not always related. So he started a career in Christian media and then became executive vice president of a financial securities/asset management firm in the northeast.

Brian then served as president of a $38 million international media non-profit in Florida before moving to Texas to become the COO of a large marketing agency. Brian moved back into the non-profit world with Online for Life in early 2012 when it blossomed into the national effort it is today.

Originally piloted in 2007, Online for Life is a transparent, metric-oriented, compassion-driven organization dedicated to rescuing babies and families from abortion through technology and grace.

Brian is the author of four books and numerous articles. His columns have appeared in publications such as FoxNews.com, the Washington Post, Crosswalk, and CBN.com. Brian and his wife, Jessica, have two sons and live in the Dallas area.